**IT'S GOT ALL THE QUESTIONS!**
**YOU SUPPLY THE ANSWERS!**

Thousands of incredibly entertaining, absurd, baroque, stupendous, ingenious questions, puzzles, rebuses et cetera, to test the mind and the alertness of a vast and entertaining audience of *Guinness* fans!

The highest, lowest, biggest, smallest, fastest, slowest, loudest, softest, hottest, coldest, oldest, newest, strongest in the whole wide wonderful world . . .

The companion book to the greatest record book of all time belongs in the home of all lovers of fun and frivolity!

MILLIONS WILL FIND THE QUESTIONS HERE—AND THE ANSWERS HERE AND THERE!

# Guinness Book of Games and Puzzles

## Devised by Norvin Pallas

Based on the 21st Edition of
GUINNESS BOOK OF RECORDS
by Norris and Ross McWhirter

CORGI BOOKS
A DIVISION OF TRANSWORLD PUBLISHERS LTD

GUINNESS BOOK OF GAMES AND PUZZLES

A CORGI/CAROUSEL BOOK 552 09750 0

First publication in Great Britain

PRINTING HISTORY
Corgi/Carousel edition published 1974


Corgi Books are published by
Transworld Publishers Ltd.,
Cavendish House, 57–59 Uxbridge Road,
Ealing, London W.5.
Made and printed in the United States of America
by Arcata Graphics,
Buffalo, New York

## CONTENTS

# INTRODUCTION

All of the quizzes, riddles, and puzzles in the *Guinness Book of Games and Puzzles* are based on information to be found in the 21st edition of the *Guinness Book of Records.* Following every question or its solution in this book is the *Guinness Book of Records* page number (in parentheses) on which each record is fully explained.

This volume has two main purposes: the first, but *not* the most important, is to test your knowledge of the thousands of records and facts, both serious and not-so-serious, contained in the *Guinness Book of Records.* The second and major purpose is to provide you with as much pleasure and enjoyment as possible. After all, a puzzle or game isn't worth the paper it's printed on if it doesn't amount to something more than a test.

When you have a little time to spare, call family and friends together (or, if you would rather, just find a quiet, comfortable spot off by yourself) and try out a few of the puzzles. Start with the simpler ones first; you can try the more difficult quizzes after you get the hang of it. If you come across a question that has you completely stumped, don't immediately look up the answer in the back of this book—try to find it in the *Guinness Book of Records.* You not only learn more but it makes the game more interesting.

# GUINNESS PARTY QUIZ

In this game, the host reads the question aloud, and the guests call out their answers—but only one guess is allowed to a person. Since the host already knows the answer, he can easily keep track of who comes the closest. The guest who comes closest but *below* the correct answer gets a token (such as a poker chip); so does the guest who comes closest above the correct answer. Any person guessing the exact number, to the nearest whole number, gets three tokens. The one winning the most tokens is declared the winner.

What is the . . .

1. Height of the tallest man? (7)
2. Weight of the heaviest man? (11)
3. Age of the oldest human? (14)
4. Length of the longest human hair? (18)
5. Length of the longest moustache? (19)
6. Length of the longest beard? (19)
7. Circumference of the largest spider web? (42)
8. Height of the highest flea jump? (44)
9. Radial spread of the largest octopus? (45–46)
10. Length of the longest worm? (46)
11. Length of the longest snake? (38)
12. Height of the tallest living tree? (50)
13. Size of the waistline of the fattest tree? (51)
14. Weight of the largest blue whale's tongue? (26)
15. Date of the earliest cuckoo in Britain? (37)
16. Height of the tallest chimney? (116)
17. Number of steps in the world's longest stairs? (132)
18. Height of the highest waterfall? (64)
19. Greatest number of stone skips (ducks and drakes) ever attained on a water surface? (226)
20. Most times anyone has been struck by lightning and survived? (228)
21. Time consumed by the longest sermon? (230)

22. Number of years in the longest adult marriage? (222)

23. Greatest weight ever raised by a human being? (335)

24. Height of the highest stilts from ankle to ground? (231)

25. Lowest height for a limbo dancer? (225)

26. Heaviest normal new-born baby? (16)

27. Year Charles Osborne started hiccoughing, until the present? (20)

28. Longest distance travelled by a message in a bottle? (228)

29. Highest shade temperature on the earth's surface? (66)

30. Lowest screen temperature on the earth's surface? (66)

(Answers on page 107)

# HYPERBOLE

Two statements in each set are true, while one is an exaggeration. Divide the participants into two teams. The monitor presents a set of questions to one of the teams. The team must reach a consensus as to which statement is wrong. If the correct answer is given the team scores a point; if not, the opposing team may score a point by choosing correctly between the two remaining answers.

1. A. There is a river under the Nile River with six times its volume. (64)
   B. An iceberg larger than Belgium was sighted. (59)
   C. A twelve-leaf clover has been found. (54)
2. A. Mehmed Ali Halici can recite 6,666 verses of the Koran from memory. (18)
   B. A bulb has been burning since 1886. (86)
   C. Frl. Marita Günther can sing all the notes on the piano. (23)
3. A. A battery has been running since 1840. (86)
   B. The highest denomination stamp was for £250. (207)
   C. Chomsong-dae, the earliest astronomical observatory, has existed since A.D. 632. (83)
4. A. A speed of nearly 50 m.p.h. has been achieved on roller skates. (314)
   B. Jesse Owens broke six world records in 45 minutes. (330)
   C. The longest flight of a homing-pigeon is about 7,000 miles. (311)
5. A. Cardinal Mezzofanti translated 114 languages. (90)
   B. Dame Arias and Rudolf Nureyev received 106 curtain calls after a performance. (225)
   C. A stress of 1,000,000,000 g. has been mechanically achieved. (85)

6. A. By surface travel only, Rusty Baillie and Barry Cliff stood on the summits of both Mount Kilimanjaro and Mount Kenya in less than 24 hours. (308)
   B. Craig Breedlove made a skid mark almost 6 miles long. (144)
   C. Richard Honeck, a prisoner for 64 years, received only three letters. (198)
7. A. Ancient Peruvians made a straight line in the ground 10 miles long. (89)
   B. H.M. Battleship *Temeraire*, though steam-powered, carried the largest sails known. (140)
   C. Lionel Luckhoo succeeded in getting 168 consecutive murder acquittals for his clients. (195)
8. A. Hardinge Giffard won election unopposed, after receiving only one vote in a previous election. (186)
   B. The longest banana split was one mile long. (204)
   C. Lake Superior contains the most fresh water of any lake. (65)
9. A. Whisky tracked his master across Australia for 2,300 miles. (339)
   B. Pepi II of ancient Egypt reigned for 91 years. (183)
   C. A Russian line carries 800,000 volts. (158)
10. A. The largest chicken ranch produces 2,000,000 eggs per day. (172)
    B. The longest military march was 6,000 miles. (192)
    C. The London earthquake of 1580 killed two people. (214)
11. A. The heaviest earthquake ever measured occurred in the United States. (56)
    B. The *Calypso* is anchored with a 5½ mile long nylon cable. (140)
    C. The *Thomas W. Lawson* had 11 masts. (140)

12. A. The United States national debt, if piled in one dollar bills, would stretch to the moon. (201)
   B. The fastest printing machine can print 30,000 lines per minute. (158)
   C. The Black Death killed 75,000,000 people. (214)
13. A. The highest high wire act occurred 1,950 feet above the ground. (341)
   B. The center span of the Fremont Bridge weighing 6,000 short tons was raised by hydraulic jack. (159)
   C. General Motors paid over $1,500 million in dividends in 1973. (164)
14. A. The world's largest vineyard covers more than 2 million acres. (172)
   B. Though his mother had over $31 million in one bank, Hetty Green's son had both his legs amputated because she delayed to find a free clinic. (234)
   C. Arthur Onslow was Mr. Speaker for 33 years. (188)
15. A. Johann Ketzler ate a whole roast ox in 28 days. (236)
   B. Sugar Ray Robinson won the same boxing title five times. (251)
   C. Eskimos play dominoes with 148 pieces. (296)
16. A. An electric eel may discharge up to 650 volts. (42)
   B. A flying fish may "fly" more than half a mile. (41)
   C. The Monaco Grand Prix requires about 3,000 gear changes. (304)
17. A. Len Smith was British marbles champion 15 times, but in 1974 lost to his son. (300)
   B. Norman Manley scored three consecutive holes-in-one. (285)
   C. Charlotte Dod was victorious at Wimbledon at age 15. (299)

18. A. Osamu Minagawa at age 6 achieved sales of 1,000,000 copies of a recording. (106)
B. Janet Aitchison at age 5½ wrote a story that was later published. (96)
C. Gino Lyons at age 4 painted a picture that was later exhibited at the Royal Academy of Arts. (88)

19. A. The highest speed for a giant tortoise is 0.17 m.p.h. (38)
B. The highest speed for a spider is 2.34 m.p.h. (43)
C. The highest speed for a snail is 0.0313 m.p.h. (46)

20. A. The highest sand dunes are 1,410 feet. (63)
B. The highest waterspout was 5,014 feet. (67)
C. The tallest iceberg was 1,100 feet above the surface. (59)

(Answers on page 108)

# TWENTY-ONE

Each of the problems below has a different answer, but each can be answered with a number between 1 and 21 inclusive. Fractions are dropped.

A. A sponge weighing up to 90 lb. weighed ____ pounds after being dried. (46)
B. Stanley Baldwin was Prime Minister ____ times. (188)
C. A cat survived a fall of ____ storeys. (35)
D. A sea hare snail weighed ____ pounds. (46)
E. The earthquake of 1884 resulted in a fatality list of ____. (56)
F. Four-horse carriages could maintain a speed of ____ m.p.h. for nearly an hour. (141)
G. The longest pea pod was ____ inches. (53)
H. A frog made a long leap of ____ feet. (40)
I. The largest tricycle could carry ____ riders. (145)
J. The longest and heaviest freight train was ____ miles. (147)
K. An angry black mamba was timed at ____ m.p.h. (39)
L. An Alsatian made a high jump of ____ feet. (34)
M. A giraffe was almost ____ feet tall. (25)
N. Jack Sholomir blew a flame ____ feet from his mouth. (21)
O. The lowest Bank of England bank rate has been ____%. (201)
P. The largest grape vine yielded ____ tons some years. (50)
Q. Janice Deveree had a beard of ____ inches. (19)
R. The most a barometer can fall is ____ inches. (68)
S. The tallest sunflower was ____ feet. (53)

(Answers on page 108)

# A BIRTHDAY TREASURE HUNT

Persons who are not easily frustrated may enjoy a birthday treasure hunt that will lead them to their gifts, thus building up suspense and postponing that golden moment. The first clue is read or given to the player. When he has solved it successfully, it will take him to the place where the next clue is hidden, and so on, until he has reached the treasure trove at the end of the trail. Given below are some possible clues from Guinness, which may be adapted to your own environment.

If you are lazy, or it isn't your birthday, you may want to play arm-chair treasure hunt. Answer each question just as though the clues really had been planted and there really is a treasure. You may not go on to the next clue until the present one has been answered correctly. A partner will tell you whether or not your guess is correct.

1. A game played by the pilgrims on the *Mayflower.* (266)
2. An invention achieved by T.A.E. (106)
3. Where will you find floccipaucinihilipilification? (91)
4. The Pentagon has 44,000 of them. (115)
5. Where Francis I hung the "Mona Lisa." (87)
6. The biggest tree would make 5,000 million of them. (50)
7. The longest match lasted 7½ hours. (296)
8. The first successful British model was built by Frederick Bremer. (141)
9. The largest U.K. prize is £5,580. (110)
10. If real, it would weigh 5.517 times as much as water. (72)
11. An unexpected feature of the smallest house in Britain. (120)
12. There may be four million of them in the United Kingdom. (38)

13. The largest one has 90,000 parts. (158)

14. It can be smashed with bare hands in 41 minutes 29 seconds. (229)

15. It was first demonstrated between two kites. (108)

16. Stonehenge may have been a ______. (130)

(Answers on page 109)

## LIMERICKS

1. Bill Fuqua was not such a dummy,
But his visits were not very chummy.
He'd sit in his chair,
And for hours he'd stare;
But it's risky to live like a dummy.

What happened to him? (21)

2. Six shillings is not such a lot,
But that is the sum that I got,
For a small paper square;
I don't thinks it was fair,
I could have been rich, but I'm not.

What was it? (208)

3. You have all heard the tale of Jack Sprat,
And how he could eat no fat,
But with Mills and wife Mary,
These things were contrary,
Now what is the reason for that? (11)

(Answers on page 109)

# A QUICKIE QUIZ

See how many of these questions you can answer correctly in fifteen minutes. Speed is the objective. Some are trick questions or puns, so do not give them too much thought.

1. What is the last name of the man who discovered Angel Falls? (64)
2. Where was badminton devised? (245)
3. Who was the first man to land on the moon? (215)
4. Why do Mr and Mrs Edward Petritz have mixed feelings about 15 April? (17)
5. What advantage do some asthmatic children have? (23)
6. In what occupation are panty hose considered quite masculine? (46)
7. Who was Howard Libbey? (50)
8. What did the Russians do to shorten the Nile River? (63)
9. What is the name of the highest lake in the world? (65)
10. What happens in Washington, D.C., when two-fifths of the sum of the dry and wet bulb thermometer readings plus 15 equals 86 or more? (66)
11. Where will you find the biggest junk? (140)
12. Why can a record set by the motor lifeboat *Intrepid* be matched but never exceeded? (140)
13. Why won't British Rail take you up Snowdon Mountain? (147)
14. What passenger reached the highest speed on rails? (148)
15. What was the name of the Wright Brothers' first plane? (148)
16. How do the British feel about the world's largest airport in Texas? (152)
17. What is heavenly about the world's largest non-hydro-electric generating plant? (154)

18. Who prints more money than the U.S. Treasury? (162)

19. What did the largest Christmas cracker conceal? (169)

20. The penknife with the most blades had how many blades in 1974? (170–171)

21. What is the name of the river on which Mexico City is situated? (181)

22. Why did Jean I of France never issue a command? (184)

23. The bloodiest civil war was the T'ai-p'ing rebellion. What does the name mean? (189)

24. If the chief cause of crime is law, which country should have the most crime? (193)

25. What would have happened to the youngest English judge if he had found the Fountain of Youth? (195)

26. Why were 1,314 people arrested on 17 September 1961? (198)

27. From whom were 398 lb. of heroin and cocaine stolen in 1973? (199)

28. Has any prisoner regained his freedom from Alcatraz? (200)

29. The earliest strike in ancient Rome was over what grievance? (203)

30. How far could you go with an Edward VIII penny? (202)

31. Why should a stout M.P. avoid Parliament Street? (206)

32. Where is a British motorist most likely to get confused? (206)

33. Where in the United Kingdom can you see the most cars? (206)

34. How does Jesse Rosdail feel about North Korea, North Vietnam, China, Cuba, and French Antarctica? (216)

35. How was the first speed record attained? (217)

36. Why would it be difficult to surpass a record set by Jacques Piccard and Donald Walsh? (220)

37. What hazard did Ken Baily face while running at night in a luminous suit? (220)

38. John Lees bettered John Ball's time in crossing contiguous United States on foot. What was most remarkable about Lees' record? (221)

39. When L. E. Chittenden signed 12,500 bonds in 48 hours, what did he get for his pains? (224)

40. What is Susan Jenkins' opinion of a spending spree in New York? (224)

41. What is the name of the largest permanent circus? (233)

42. What invention made Annie Malone a millionairess? (234)

43. What is the largest object named after a man? (236)

44. What contretemps faced spectators at an Aztec basketball game? (246)

45. Where could you hit a golf ball a mile on level ground? (283)

46. The heaviest ocean sunfish weighed 2.24 tons. How was it caught? (41)

47. Why was it a good thing for Gigi that she didn't diet? (55)

48. The Zeus capacitor could generate twice as much current as the rest of the world combined. But what's the catch? (85)

49. What are the following letters: A B E G I K O P R T U? (90)

50. Charles Zibbelman holds the record for endurance swimming; what is most remarkable about his record? (221)

51. Why is there a reasonable doubt about the first person swimming from England to France?

(Answers on pages 110–111)

# PAINTING LADDER

The "Mona Lisa" is the world's most valuable painting. Can you change MONA to LISA by changing just one letter at a time? Each line must spell a word. (87)

| | | | |
|---|---|---|---|
| M | O | N | A |
| | | | |
| | | | |
| | | | |
| | | | |
| | | | |
| L | I | S | A |

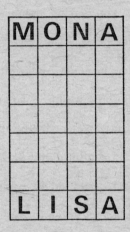

(Answer on page 112)

# SPEED LADDER

The fastest moving animal is believed to be a bird, the spine-tailed swift, while the animal most noted for its slowness is the snail. Can you change SWIFT to SNAIL by changing just one letter at a time? Each line must spell a word. (37, 28)

| | | | | |
|---|---|---|---|---|
| S | W | I | F | T |
| | | | | |
| | | | | |
| | | | | |
| | | | | |
| | | | | |
| | | | | |
| | | | | |
| S | N | A | I | L |

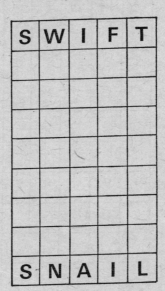

(Answer on page 112)

# MAMMAL LADDER

Can you change the largest mammal into the smallest mammal by changing just one letter at a time? Each line must spell a word. (25, 28)

| | | | | |
|---|---|---|---|---|
| W | H | A | L | E |
| | | | | |
| | | | | |
| | | | | |
| | | | | |
| | | | | |
| | | | | |
| | | | | |
| | | | | |
| | | | | |
| | | | | |
| | | | | |
| | | | | |
| S | H | R | E | W |

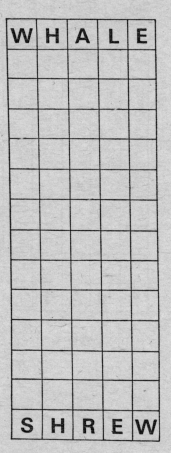

(Answer on page 112)

# LETTER CROSS OUT

Example: Albert Einstein was a great ______. (74)

TH~~EGU~~IN~~NESSBOO~~K~~OFR~~E~~CO~~R~~DS~~

1. Juan Belmonte was ______ 50 times. (253)

THEGUINNESSBOOKOFRECORDS

2. The oldest ______ food was roast beef. (205)

THEGUINNESSBOOKOFRECORDS

3. When Chang ______ to ______ Eng does ______. (16)

THEGUINNESSBOOKOFRECORDS

THEGUINNESSBOOKOFRECORDS

THEGUINNESSBOOKOFRECORDS

4. A white shark is the largest fish ever ______. (241)

THEGUINNESSBOOKOFRECORDS

5. ______ Trueman has taken the greatest number of wickets in Test matches. (259)

THEGUINNESSBOOKOFRECORDS

6. Eddie Masher was known for his ______. (11)

THEGUINNESSBOOKOFRECORDS

7. A production record was set by a Black Orpington ______. (173)

THEGUINNESSBOOKOFRECORDS

8. The most massive ______ even constructed was the "Schwerer Gustav." (191)

THEGUINNESSBOOKOFRECORDS

9. ______ produced the most popular car model, until the Volkswagen "Beetle." (142)

THEGUINNESSBOOKOFRECORDS

10. Anthony Moreno was a ______ with 3,000 "children." (200)

THEGUINNESSBOOKOFRECORDS

11. Arthur Blore was a ______ who uniquely won the Conspicuous Gallantry Medal and bar. (237)

THEGUINNESSBOOKOFRECORDS

12. "The Trip to Jerusalem" might be the United Kingdom's oldest ______. (121)

THEGUINNESSBOOKOFRECORDS

13. David Kwan made a record ______ through 14 countries. (227)

THEGUINNESSBOOKOFRECORDS

14. The Ch'ient'ang'kian has the world's most remarkable ______. (64)

THEGUINNESSBOOKOFRECORDS

15. Loch ______ has the greatest mean depth in Great Britain. (65)

THEGUINNESSBOOKOFRECORDS

(Answers on page 112)

# SETS

Tell what the members of each set have in common.

1. Pitcairn Island.
   Ducie Island.
   Cape Dart, Antarctica. (58)
2. The Defaulter.
   Squire of Malton.
   Reindeer.
   Pulcherrima. (290)
3. Overreach.
   Lady Go-Lightly.
   Gamester.
   The Unexpected. (290)
4. Ooqueah.
   Egingwah.
   Seegloo.
   Ootah. (218)
5. Gene Tunney.
   Rocky Marciano. (251)
6. *Morning Glory.*
   *Guess Who's Coming to Dinner.*
   *The Lion in Winter.* (108)
7. *St. Louis Blues.*
   *Stardust.* (106)
8. Tsu-chin. (269)
   Pula. (311)
   Pok-ta-Pok. (246)
   Whist. (295)
   Chaturanga. (255)
   Paganica. (281)
   Baggataway. (298)
9. Laurasia.
   Gondwanaland. (59)
10. Tristan da Cunha.
    Bouvert Øya. (60)

11. Evitative.
Redivider.
Malayalam. (91)
12. Anticonstitutionnellement.
Prijestolenaslijeduikovice.
Precipitevolissimevolmente.
Ryāgū-no-otohime-no-motoyui-no-kirihazushi.
Ryentgyenoelyektrokardiografichyeskogo.
Engedelmeskedhetetlenségeskedéseitekert. (92)
13. Octavio Guillen.
Adriana Martinez. (222)
14. Regis Toomey.
Jane Wyman. (228)
15. *Baby's Breakfast.*
*Lunch Hour at the Lumière Factory.*
*The Arrival of a Train.* (108)
16. Fulton Berley.
Bert Henry.
Betty Taylor. (105)
17. Olekminsk.
Verkhoyansk. (67)
18. Toro.
Amor.
Eros.
Ivar. (72)
19. Proxima Centauri.
Alpha Centauri. (73)
20. Gerald Carr.
William Pogue.
Edward Gibson. (75–76)
21. E.
J.
M.
X. (94)
22. ?
! (97)
23. *Yamato.*
*Musashi.* (138)
24. John Bardeen.

Walter Brattain.
R. L. Wallace.
Morgan Sparks.
William Shockley. (159)

25. Phillumenists.
Philliberumenists.
Cumyxaphists. (170)
26. John Addison.
Alexander Rowley. (186)
27. Otto Hahn.
Fritz Strassman.
Lise Meitner. (192)
28. *R. v. Murray.*
*R. v. Cawley.* (193)
29. Money in Laos.
Money in Paraguay. (202)
30. Imbibers in Iceland.
Imbibers in the U.S.S.R.
Imbibers in the United States. (204)
31. Tapon del Darién.
Atrato Swamp. (206)
32. James Lovell.
Frederick Haise.
John Swigert. (215)
33. Miyeko Mori.
Masako Uchida.
Naoko Kuribayashi. (219)
34. Dyura Avramovich.
Yula Zhivich. (222)
35. Rosemarie Frankland.
Ann Sidney.
Lesley Langley. (226)
36. 8 duchesses.
15 marchionesses.
21 countesses.
19 Spanish grandees. (236)
37. Arthur Martin-Leake.
Noel Chavasse.
Charles Upham. (236)

38. George Cross.
    Conspicuous Gallantry Medal (Flying).
    Queen's Gallantry Medal. (237)
39. *The Star of Africa.*
    *The Star of Sierra Leone.* (81)
40. Ormonde. (290)
    Sceptre. (291)
41. Watling Street.
    Fosse Way. (206)

(Answers on pages 113–114)

# BRAIN TEASER

Take the mass of the earth in tons, rounding off the last 18 places . . . (56)

Multiply it by the distance in miles, rounding off the last 12 places, to the nearest star (other than the sun) . . . (73)

Divide by the surface area of the oceans, rounded off to the nearest million square miles . . . (58)

Add the total gold mined from Crown Mines, South Africa, in ounces, rounding off the last six places . . . (135)

Subtract the United Kingdom's national debt, rounded off to the nearest million pounds . . . (201)

Multiply by the feet above sea level of the highest crater on the moon . . . (70)

And divide by the gross national product of the U.S.A. for 1972, rounding off the dollars to the last eight places.

Your answer__________________

(Answer on page 114)

## RIDDLES

1. Of the Chinese I proudly sing,
   Fifty-two strokes and call it "ping." (90)
2. I learned my letters from A to Z.
   How many more could I have in my head? (90)
3. Rings around me, I'm no boat,
   If I had water enough I'd float. (72)
4. Buddy, Buddy, struck it Rich,
   Beat the band, but had no pitch. (102)
5. Here is a riddle you may guess:
   What are London and Paris on Christmas? (60)
6. Five thousand feet long, it made a good show,
   But the Father of Waters no more will unroll. (87)
7. An expert surgeon, goodness knows,
   But count your fingers, count your toes. (24)
8. Oh, Devon Smith can now rejoice:
   Six thousand tries to roll in a Royce. (227)
9. I could do fine, the prospect lingers,
   If only I had six thousand fingers. (232)
10. He was, he claimed, a used furniture dealer,
    Made a hundred million a year as a "stealer." (234)
11. Father and daughter were a perfect fit,
    So they rode through the air without minding a bit. (227)
12. Good marriages may be made in heaven,
    But Kathy's tiers were twenty-seven. (204)
13. Joe Thomas had a rare inside,
    That made him Internal Revenue's pride. (19)
14. If you want to see a show,
    See the gallery of Sailor Joe. (20)
15. Veronica Seider, with open eye,
    Was twenty times better than you or I. (22)

(Answers on page 115)

# STRANGE JOURNEYS

1. In what special way did a Russian go from Tyuratam to Smelovka? (75)

2. How did Samuel Brown negotiate Shooters Hill? (141)

3. In what unique way did Ben and Elinore Carlin cross the Atlantic? (144)

4. How did Steve McPeak go from Chicago to Las Vegas, 2,000 miles? (145)

5. How did H. Berliner go from Bitterfeld, Germany, to Kirgishan, U.S.S.R., 1,896 miles? (153)

6. How did Matt Wiederker go from St. Paul, Minnesota, to Butte, Iowa, 334 miles? (154)

7. How did John Potter make 1,171 yards the hard way? (154)

8. Where did Ralph Plaisted and companions Skidoo for 42 days? (218)

9. How did Plennie Wingo go from Forth Worth, Texas, to Istanbul, Turkey, 8,000 miles on land? (221)

10. How did Fred Newton go from Minneapolis to New Orleans, 1,826 miles? (221)

11. How did Clarence Giles go from Glendive to Billings, Montana, 228 miles in 71 hours? (221)

12. How did William Willis go from Peru to Western Samoa, 7,450 miles? (221)

13. How did Pam Vere and Georgina Astley go from Land's End to John o' Groats, 873 miles in less than a day? (227)

14. How did William Becker travel 1,600 yards, ending in a tree? (227)

15. How did Bill Bennett get from Dante's Peak to Death Valley, 6.2 miles? (228)

16. How did Sylvain Dornon go from Paris to Moscow, 1,830 miles? (231)

17. How did Charles Blondin cross the U.S.–Canada border? (232)

18. How did Johann Hurlinger go from Vienna to Paris, 871 miles? (232)

19. How did Geoffrey Pope and Sheldon Taylor go from New York City to Nome, Alaska, 7,165 miles? (254)

20. How did David Ryder go from Los Angeles to New York City, 2,960 miles? (334)

21. When Floyd Rood crossed contiguous United States, why did he pause 114,737 times? (281)

22. What was remarkable about Geofrey Bull's covering 100 yards in a record 11 seconds? (332)

23. How did dancer Bill Robinson cover 100 yards in a record 13.5 seconds? (331)

24. How did Simon Paterson cross from France to England in 14 hours 50 minutes? (324)

25. How did Fred Baldasare cross from France to England in 18 hours 1 minute? (324)

26. How did Rick Sylvester get down from the sheer face of El Capitan in California? (319)

27. How did Sylvian Squdan get down from Mount McKinley, the highest peak in the United States? (319)

28. How did Clinton Shaw cross from Victoria, British Columbia, to St. John's, Newfoundland? (315)

(Answers on page 116)

# SCENIC ACROSTIC

If you fill in the correct letters horizontally, the two ringed vertical columns will give the name of a natural wonder of the world. (64)

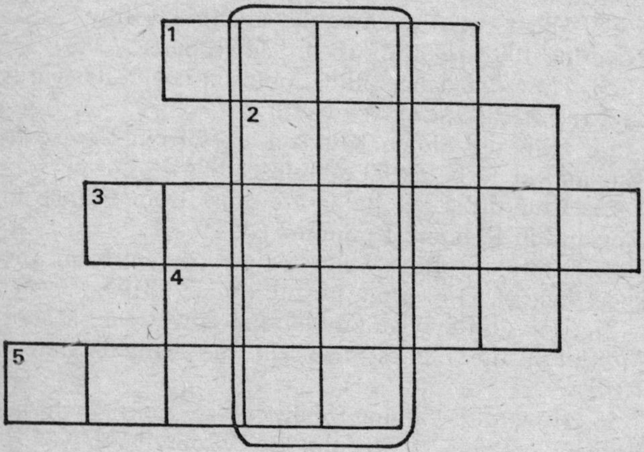

1. Poon Lim survived 133 days alone on a ______. (221)
2. En-lil-ti might be the first known personal ______. (93)
3. ______ is the most widely spoken language. (90)
4. Loughborough, Leicestershire, is well known for its ______. (103)
5. David Bryant won or shared 12 ______ championships. (249)

(Answers on page 117)

# SPORTS ACROSTIC

If you fill in the correct letters horizontally, the two ringed vertical columns will spell out the name of a record-holding athlete. (269)

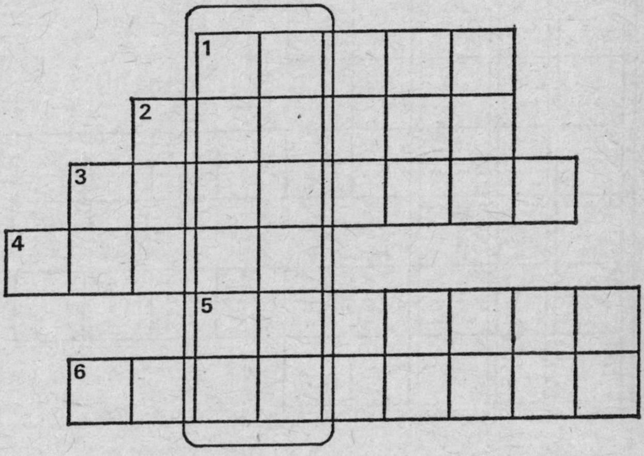


1. Thunder Bay, Ontario, Canada, is a great ______ center. (117)
2. The greatest meteor display was the ______. (69)
3. Tide Lake, British Columbia, Canada, had the greatest annual ______. (68)
4. The largest ______ was found in a clam. (81)
5. ______ built the largest rigid airship. (153)
6. Sherry's Prince is a famous ______. (286)

(Answers on page 117)

# GIANT ACROSTIC

If you fill in the correct letters horizontally, the two ringed vertical columns will spell out the name of a giant. (7)

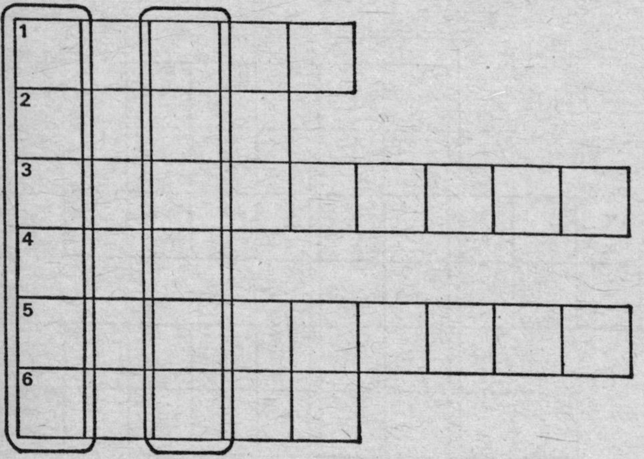

1. How did John Fairfax cross the Atlantic in 180 days? (219)
2. A bulldozer at Andamooka uncovered what large semiprecious stone? (81)
3. What game uses a cork that can be driven over 79 feet? (245)
4. An electric _______ can deliver 650 volts. (42)
5. What politician nicknamed Teddy shook hands with 8,513 people in one day? (227)
6. Emley Moor has the tallest _______ in the United Kingdom. (123)

(Answers on page 117)

# THE BEGINNING AND THE END

From the start and the finish, tell what event is described.

| | *Start* | *Finish* | |
|---|---|---|---|
| 1. | Denise Darvall | Louis Washkansky | (24) |
| 2. | Signal Hill, St. John's, Newfoundland | Poldhu, Cornwall | (109) |
| 3. | Les Baraques, France | Northfall Meadow, England | (148) |
| 4. | Trespassey Harbour, Newfoundland | Lisbon, Portugal | (149) |
| 5. | St. John's, Newfoundland | Derrygimla Bog, County Galway | (149) |
| 6. | Empire State Building, New York | Post Office Tower, London | (149) |
| 7. | The Thames | Lake Havasu City, Arizona | (168) |
| 8. | Barealdine, Queensland | Beaconsfield Station, Queensland | (172) |
| 9. | Point Barrow, Alaska | Seven Island Archipelago | (218) |
| 10. | Las Palmas, Canary Islands | Fort Lauderdale, Florida | (219) |

(Answers on page 118)

# YES OR NO SPELLDOWN

This game is conducted like an old-fashioned spelling bee. Two teams are chosen, and the monitor addresses a question alternately to a player on one team, and then the other. A player missing a question must sit down, until an entire team has been eliminated.

1. Is *The Week's Good Cause* the most durable B.B.C. radio series? (109)
2. Are there more than ten specimens of taaffeite known? (82)
3. Is it possible to motor up Pike's Peak in ten minutes? (305)
4. Was "Kill Van Kull" a political slogan of early settlers in New Amsterdam? (124)
5. Is Mauna Loa the tallest mountain as measured from its submarine base? (63)
6. Has an adder longer than a yard been found in Britain? (39)
7. Is the world's longest road tunnel under the Matterhorn? (128)
8. Is the earth longer around the equator than around the poles? (56)
9. Would the highest mountain fit into the deepest part of the ocean? (61, 58)
10. Are rubies used in laser technology? (81)
11. Is the oldest living tree named Joshua? (339)
12. Is Windsor Castle the world's largest inhabited castle? (118)
13. Does the largest temple in the world honour Buddha? (210)
14. Is the oldest known song a military march? (100)
15. Was the largest mined stone placed in the Temple of Athene? (135)
16. Is tabasco the hottest spice? (205)
17. Does the tallest woman live in India? (9)
18. Does the coypu live wild in Britain? (31)

19. Are there more chickens in the world than people? (36)

20. Was Great Britain the first country to defeat the Japanese in karate competition? (297)

21. Has the United States held the Davis Cup the longest? (300)

22. Is the biggest rodeo held in the United States? (314)

23. Have trotters set better record times than pacers? (332)

24. Is the standing long jump more than twice the distance of the record standing high jump? (332)

25. Is the word I used more in conversation than the word you? (91)

26. Is the twin sister of Don Koehler, the tallest living man, over six feet tall? (8)

27. Can an arrow be shot farther than the height of the tallest building? (244)

28. Is the most numerous tree in the largest forest the oak? (52)

29. Is there a hundred times as much salt water as fresh water? (58)

30. Did the Crown of Thorns win a national flower contest? (60)

31. Is the summit of Mount Everest the farthest from the centre of the earth? (61)

32. Is London the foggiest place in the world? (68)

33. Is Pendennis Castle the sunniest place in the British Isles? (68)

34. Is the Aurora Borealis visible at the equator? (70)

35. Does the earth rotate the fastest of any major planet? (71)

36. Is the galaxy in Orion the remotest heavenly body visible with the unaided eye? (74)

37. Will Pioneer X leave the Solar System? (75)

38. Is LSD the most powerful drug? (80)

39. Does the earliest known vellum document contain work of Demosthenes? (94)

40. Is *The Little Drummer Boy* the best-selling L.P.? (107)

41. Was *West Side Story* the film with the most Oscars? (108)

42. Could the car of the President of the United States travel at 50 m.p.h. with four flat tyres? (142)

43. Does St. Paul's Cathedral have the longest land tenure? (166)

44. Is vicuña the finest cloth? (169)

45. Did the U.S.S.R. have the highest percentage of casualties in World War II? (189)

46. Is the Swiss army the oldest? (190)

47. Were more people killed in the London fire of 1666 than in the London Bridge fire? (214)

48. Is Richmond Castle the oldest stone castle extant in Great Britain? (117)

49. Did the earliest known English patent concern boot polish? (193)

50. Do cats live longer than dogs? (35)

51. Did King George IV appear on the first adhesive postage stamps? (207)

(Answers on pages 118–119)

# WHAT'S THE QUESTION?

Here is a group of answers. But what are the questions to fit the answers?

1. *Chicago* and *New Orleans.* (149)
2. She said that five of them broke her nose. (221–222)
3. Church organs and libraries. (235)
4. She could be used as a spy in peacetime but was too vulnerable in wartime. (153)
5. A jail cell, three handcuffs, footcuffs, chains, and a thick window. (226)
6. By a host of starlings for five minutes. (158)
7. Borley Rectory. (24)
8. *The Battle of Gettysburg.* (87)
9. *Mr and Mrs Gravenor and their daughters Elizabeth and Dorothea.* (87)
10. "London Daily Mail." (91)
11. READYMIX. (91)
12. *Chattanooga Choo Choo.* (106)
13. *Panorama.* (110)
14. Temple of Horyu. (117)
15. Sadd al-Kafara. (126)
16. Bertha Rogers. (133)
17. Randfontein Estates. (135)
18. Because the insurance rates go up as she goes down. (138)
19. It runs a snuff mill. (156)
20. The Unknown Soldier. (82)
21. Marble Arch. (162)
22. It broke the most priceless occidental ceramic. (170)
23. Friends of the Moon. (185)
24. Culloden Field. (188)
25. Carreg Gwastad. (189)
26. Vše zene. (195)
27. There was a strike for 33 years. (203)
28. Hard Knott Pass. (206)

29. Holme Fen. (207)
30. By the submarine *Alvin.* (220)
31. 1,792. (123)
32. The River Meles. (123)
33. Llansantffraed Cwmdauddwr. (54)
34. 80 miles on the ground, 300 miles from aircraft. (131)
35. Lava Falls. (64)
36. *Lights of New York.* (108)
37. *The Little Red Elf.* (94)
38. Button Gwinnett. (98)
39. It has legally existed "from time immemorial." (160)
40. Pico de Veleta. (206)
41. *Long Lines.* (139)
42. 007. (108)
43. Coffee Club. (60)
44. The *Silver Wink.* (326)
45. You must quack and have web feet. (321)
46. Because they have no words. (102)

(Answers on pages 120–121)

# MATCH THE ANSWERS

Match the number of each statement to the letter of the correct answer.

1. Largest flying creature (extinct). (47)
2. Mountain peak farthest from the centre of the earth. (61)
3. Tallest racing horse in Britain. (33)
4. Highest separate unclimbed mountain. (63)
5. Mightiest waterfall (annual flow basis). (64)
6. Largest meteorite exhibited. (69)
7. Birthplace of Neil Armstrong. (215)
8. Oldest brewery. (162)

9. Lighthouse with the most powerful light. (131)
10. May be the largest gas field discovered. (134)
11. Most prolific wildcat gusher. (134)
12. Earliest machinery still in use. (156)
13. Most primitive cheeses. (174)
14. Highest town in the world. (181)
15. Earliest known judicial code. (192)
16. The greatest ransom historically was paid for him—futilely. (199)

A. Abnighito.
B. Atahualpa.
C. Chimborazo.
D. Créac'h d'Ouessant.
E. Dâlu.
F. Fort d'Or.
G. Gasherbrum III.
H. Groningen.
I. Guairá.
J. Kishk.
K. Pteranodon.
L. Spindletop.
M. Urnammu.
N. Wapakoneta.
O. Weihenstephan.
P. Wenchuan.

(Answers on page 122)

# TRUE/PLUS/MINUS

If you believe the statement is true, circle the T. If you believe it is false and should be higher, circle the plus sign; if you think the correct figure should be lower, circle the minus sign.

1. A plant in Bolivia, *Puya raimondii*, takes 90 years to bloom. (52) T + —
2. A rhododendron of Nepal may reach 60 feet. (53) T + —
3. The Warszawa Radio Mast is 1,350 feet tall. (122) T + —
4. Piling for the Ponte de Salazar reaches down 390 feet. (125) T + —
5. The longest irrigation tunnel is 78 miles. (128) T + —
6. Tides in the Bay of Fundy reach 87 feet. (59) T + —
7. The longest horse race is 1,200 miles. (290) T + —
8. The most horses in a race is 44. (291) T + —
9. The longest regular ice skating race is 124 miles. (294) T + —
10. The longest game of draughts lasted 5 hours. (296) T + —
11. The motorcycling speed record is 224 m.p.h. (302) T + —
12. A mountaineer survived a slide of 12,000 feet. (308) T + —
13. The highest speed in a power boat is 147 m.p.h. (312) T + —
14. The longest ski-jump is 554 feet. (318) T + —
15. The longest chair lift is 2 miles (319) T + —
16. The longest surf ride is a little over a mile. (321) T + —
17. The longest distance run in 24 hours is 248 miles. (331) T + —

18. The longest distance walked in 24 hours is 133 miles. (334) T + –

19. The longest jump on water skis is 116 feet. (334) T + –

20. The United States has held the America's Cup for 73 years. (338) T + –

21. Brothers were found after being separated for 68 years. (341) T + –

22. The tallest flagstaff was 469 feet. (129) T + –

23.The greatest load shifted by a dog is 7,400 lb. (34) T + –

24. The largest drum is 18 feet in diameter. (101) T + –

25. The deepest permafrost is 3,117 feet. (67) T + –

26. A British expedition used 18,000 feet of rope to climb Annapurna I. (306) T + –

27. The longest power boat jump is 165 feet. (313) T + –

28. Don Davis plays 9 instruments at once. (223) T + –

29. The longest fibre rope without a splice was 11 miles. (171) T + –

30. The longest railway run is 3,162 miles. (146) T + –

31. The longest straight railway track is 297 miles. (146) T + –

32. The fastest speed by a steam locomotive is 193 m.p.h. (146) T + –

33. The largest tyres are 19 feet in diameter. (144) T + –

34. The lowest body temperature any human has survived is 60°F. (20) T + –

35. The longest sword swallowed is 15 inches. (21) T + –

36. The oldest elephant was 94 years. (28) T + –

37. The longest feather was 22 feet. (37) T + –

38. Unprotected men have endured a temperature of 400°F. (22) T + —

39. The tallest barbers pole is 50 feet. (133) T + —

40. The longest day's run by a sailing ship was 301 nautical miles. (140) T + —

41. A conveyance called "Atlas" has 116 wheels. (144) T + —

42. The largest excavator has a grab of 375 tons. (156) T + —

43. A wheel in a celestial clock takes 15,000 years to make one full circle. (159) T + —

44. The most finely woven carpet has about 2,500 knots per in². (168) T + —

45. Britain's foot-and-mouth disease of 1967–68 led to the slaughter of 275,000 animals. (174) T + —

46. Edmund Waller was elected to Parliament at the age of 15. (187) T + —

47. In the 19th century there were 142 capital crimes. (197) T + —

48. A postman in Spain was sentenced for failing to deliver 25,000 letters. (198) T + —

49. The longest traffic jam in Britain was 17 miles. (207) T + —

50. Wilma Williams attended 415 different schools. (210) T + —

51. James Boucher was a schoolmaster 72 years. (210) T + —

52. The greatest pile-up in Britain involved 300 vehicles. (214) T + —

53. The greatest distance walked nonstop is 477 miles. (221) T + —

54. Polly Gadsby worked at the same job for 86 years. (222) T + —

55. The longest boomerang throw is 215 feet. (224) T + —

56. The highest dive is 475 feet. (227) T + —

57. A train of kites has flown over 6 miles high. (228) T + −

58. 45 skydivers made the biggest star. (229) T + −

59. A pipe was kept lit on one match for 2½ hours. (229) T + −

60. St. Daniel spent 22 years on a stone pillar. (229) T + −

61. The record for projecting a melon seed is 82 feet. (231) T + −

62. 653 people have sat in a circle upon each other's lap. (232) T + −

63. The youngest V.C. winner was 23 years. (236) T + −

64. The youngest woman to receive the George Cross was 27 years. (236) T + −

65. Charles Brandon was a duke for only 30 minutes. (239) T + −

66. Alfred Reed was 98 years old when he became a knight. (239) T + −

67. Joe Louis was heavyweight champion for 17 years, including war years. (251) T + −

68. The highest bicycle speed is 140 m.p.h. (263) T + −

69. Tommy Moore shot a hole-in-one at age 9. (286) T + −

70. The longest golf drive is 445 yards. (283) T + −

(Answers on pages 122–123)

# SQUARE OF FAME

Answer each clue, and then find the name spelled out in the big square, both first and last names. Names go from one block to the next in any direction except diagonally. No names appear completely on a straight line. Each letter in the square is used only once.

For example: Lloyd George

| | | | | |
|---|---|---|---|---|
| A | L | B | C | D |
| E | L | O | F | G |
| H | I | Y | D | G |
| J | K | E | O | E |
| L | N | G | R | N |

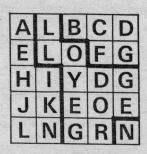

1. Has longest entry in *Who's Who.* (239)
2. Most famous baseball player. (246)
3. First to suggest an artificial satellite. (75)
4. Artist whose work brought the highest price during his lifetime. (88)
5. Most famous escape artist. (226)
6. Heaviest world champion boxer. (250)
7. First woman to swim the English Channel. (324)
8. Made first solo trans-Atlantic flight. (149)
9. First woman in space. (75, 215)
10. Attained fastest speed by a woman pilot. (215)
11. One of the first to reach the summit of Mount Everest. (219, 306)
12. Had largest human brain known. (18)
13. Famous British Antarctic explorer. (57)
14. Astronomer known for a comet. (71)
15. Took earliest photograph. (83)
16. Longest lived Poet Laureate. (96)
17. Trained animal worth £35,000. (26)
18. Sent the most Christmas cards. (98)

| | | | | | | | | | | | | | | |
|---|---|---|---|---|---|---|---|---|---|---|---|---|---|---|
| E | N | Y | A | H | K | Z | N | L | L | S | I | V | A | L |
| V | E | G | R | O | R | I | E | T | I | A | N | E | N | E |
| S | E | L | U | N | G | N | R | C | H | A | C | W | T | I |
| L | I | R | T | N | A | W | U | H | C | V | A | T | A | N |
| E | N | A | H | C | V | I | T | O | N | O | N | O | T | E |
| D | D | B | E | J | I | N | S | E | C | K | H | S | E | R |
| M | U | N | R | A | C | Q | O | S | P | E | I | N | D | R |
| R | A | D | G | L | E | U | J | E | P | H | N | I | H | A |
| R | H | H | H | I | N | E | N | M | E | S | O | X | C | I |
| Y | H | A | L | L | O | C | A | A | O | R | N | E | G | R |
| D | O | U | D | E | C | H | R | J | S | R | T | R | R | L |
| L | I | N | I | Y | A | B | R | I | S | U | E | D | E | E |
| E | A | M | O | H | P | L | P | M | O | D | E | R | E | B |
| I | R | U | J | N | O | O | P | I | C | N | E | U | T | A |
| F | E | S | A | M | S | S | A | C | A | R | R | A | H | B |

(Answers on pages 124–125)

# A HIGH I.Q. TEST

1. Conceding that Australia is a continent rather than an island, why is there some doubt that Greenland is the largest island in the world? (60)

2. What long-range problem must be considered in connection with the harnessing of the tides to generate electrical power? (155)

3. What special problem does the moon's tidal drag create for scientists? (84)

4. It is said that the two towers on the Verrazano-Narrows Bridge are not in parallel. Is this true? (123)

5. Is the earth growing lighter or heavier, or neither? (56)

6. There is some doubt that either Robert Peary or Frederick Cook reached the exact North Pole. Couldn't this be proved by a subsequent expedition that might find some indestructible memento of a previous expedition? That was how Scott discovered that Amundsen beat him to the South Pole. (218)

7. Is a tree the oldest living thing known? (54)

8. What is the oldest dated object on earth? (69)

9. Which planet, Neptune or Pluto, is farther from the sun? Explain your answer. (72)

10. Of what use is the loudest laboratory noise? (85)

11. Why is the search for tachyon particles, supposedly travelling beyond the speed of light, so difficult? (77)

12. The fraction $^{22}/_{7}$ is a reasonable approximation of pi. If this fraction is turned into a decimal, it will extend indefinitely. Could you memorise this decimal to a million places? (18)

(Answers on page 126)

# CHARADES

The monitor reads the sentence aloud, leaving out the parenthetical expression. Only the contestant is told the secret word or words, which he will try to act out until someone in the group guesses correctly.

1. The Oscar awards are named after Oscar (PIERCE). (108)

2. Michael (WALKER) had the greatest weight ever attributed to a human. (10–11)

3. Robert (HUGHES—hews) had the highest undisputed weight for a human. (11)

4. (DOLLY) (DIMPLES) was a circus fat lady who lost 401 lb. (12)

5. Dolly (WAGER) lost over 20 st. (12)

6. Charles (HUNTER) set a record for rapid speaking. (24)

7. James (YOUNG—baby) had Europe's longest-running one-man show. (105)

8. The 2nd Earl (RUSSELL—rustle) had the original A1 car registration plate. (141)

9. Maurice (FOX) won 10 consecutive national ballroom dancing title. (225)

10. Sir Francis (COOK) was married seven times. (222)

11. The Hon. Wilfrid (STAMP) legally survived his father by a split second. (239)

12. Masuriya (DIN—noise) had the world's longest moustache. (19)

13. Tom (KING) put the lowest note into song. (23)

14. George (FERRIS—wheel) invented an amusement named after himself. (121)

15. Jared R. (BEADS) ran 121 miles non-stop. (220)

16. George (LITTLEWOOD) ran 623 miles in six days. (220)

17. William F. (HARRAH—hurrah) has the greatest collection of vintage cars. (142)

18. Leslie R. V. (BURWOOD—burr, wood) toured the London Transport stations in 15 hours. (147)

19. Kurt (CANNON) attained 220 m.p.h. in a helicopter. (152)

20. Jesse (BOOT) founded the largest chain of chemist shops. (162)

21. Boyd (TAYLOR—tailor) drove his 1936 Ford a million miles. (141)

22. Orville Wright made his first flight near (KILL) (DEVIL) (HILL) at (KITTY) (HAWK). (148)

## COMPLETE THE SET

1. Charcoal, saltpetre, and ______. (74)
2. Exxon, General Motors, Ford Motor Co., and ______. (160)
3. Reindeer, goat, dog, sheep, pig and cattle, and ______. (172)
4. Norway, Finland, Poland, Czechoslovakia, Hungary, Romania, Turkey, Iran, Afghanistan, Mongolia, North Korea, and ______. (179)
5. Upper Volta, Burundi, and ______. (201)
6. Eggs stuffed in fish stuffed in chickens stuffed in sheep stuffed in ______. (204)
7. Foil, epée, and ______. (268)
8. Huarco, Toro, Santiago, Apurímac, Ene, Tambo, Ucayali, and ______. (63)
9. English Channel, Palk Strait, Straits of Gibraltar, the length of the Dardanelles, and ______. (323–324)

(Answers on page 127)

# ZERO QUIZ GAME

Zeroes appear to be nothing, but they are actually very important. Often very large numbers are rounded off with a string of zeroes at the end. That is because the exact number would be too hard to obtain, or such accuracy would serve no useful purpose. But if you add just one zero too many, your answer will be ten times too large. If you omit just one zero, your answer will be only a tenth as large as it should be.

In the following quiz, the numbers given are reasonably accurate, except that you must decide how many zeroes, if any, to add to them.

1. Warren C. Jyrich required 24____ pints of blood for an operation. (19)
2. Dentist Giovanni Orsenigo in his lifetime pulled more than 2____ teeth. (22)
3. A normal eye can detect 1____ different colour surfaces. (23)
4. A female deep-sea angler fish may weigh 5____ times as much as the male. (26)
5. A rabbit named Chewer fathered 4____ offspring. (36)
6. The ocean sunfish may produce 3____ eggs. (42)
7. A relay of bees can cruise 4____ miles on a gallon of nectar. (44)
8. A swarm of locusts may have contained 25____ insects. (44)
9. There are about 5____ detectable earthquakes annually. (56)
10. It is estimated that an avalanche in the Alps contained 35____ cubic miles of snow. (66)
11. There are about 42____ lightning strikes over Greater London annually. (67)
12. A meteorite which fell in Arizona is estimated to have weighed 2____ tons. (70)

13. A sunspot covered about 7_____ square miles. (71)

14. A comet's tail may trail for 2_____ miles. (71)

15. Comet 1910a may return in about 4_____ years. (71)

16. There are some 45_____ asteroids. (72)

17. There are 39_____ known and named chemical compounds. (71)

18. The most powerful telescope can detect the light from a candle at a distance of 15_____ miles. (82)

19. The largest dish radio telescope has a range of 15_____ light-years. (82)

20. The number 1_____ is called a Googol. (84)

21. The revolution of the sun through the Milky Way galaxy requires some 225_____ years. (84)

22. The highest man-made rotary speed is 15_____ revolutions per second. (85)

23. The magnification of a microscope can now approach 2_____ diameters. (85)

24. The heaviest magnet weighs 36_____ tons. (86)

25. A laser may be 5_____ times as bright as the sun. (86)

26. The most powerful searchlight had a maximum beam intensity of 27_____ candles. (86)

27. There are 75_____ people named Chang. (94)

28. *Old Moore's Almanack* has sold 1_____ copies. (100)

29. The largest church organ has 16_____ pipes. (100)

30. Bing Crosby has sold 362_____ records. (106)

31. 1_____ people saw the XXth Olympic Games in Munich on television. (110)

32. The Celestial Suite cost £1_____ a day. (119)

33. Wentworth Woodhouse has 1_____ windows. (120)

34. A field kitchen in India has served 12_____ meals a day. (120)

35. Southend Pier has 75_____ lamps. (121)

36. The oldest clock has ticked 5_____ times. (158)

37. The most powerful computer can perform 36____ operations in a second. (159)

38. International Business Machines had $38____ cash in the bank. (162)

39. The largest life assurance policy was for £1____. (163)

40. A mineral water firm produces 18____ bottles a year. (164)

41. The largest street carnival float has 65____ mirrors. (170)

42. The largest turkey farm has up to 12____ turkeys. (172)

43. The world's population increases by 208____ daily. (180)

44. Andorra's defence budget was £2____. (190)

45. Being wrongfully imprisoned for three years has been worth £1____. (193)

46. A three-year-old boy, if he lives long enough, may eventually receive $21____ for personal injury damages. (194)

47. The largest damage suit filed was for $675____. (194)

48. The largest swindle involved $175____. (200)

49. The highest price paid in auction for a single coin is $2____. (202)

50. M. V. Lomonosov State University, Moscow, has 4____ rooms. (209)

51. The biggest crowd contained 5____ people. (213)

52. A toy balloon has gone 9____ miles. (223)

(Answers on page 127)

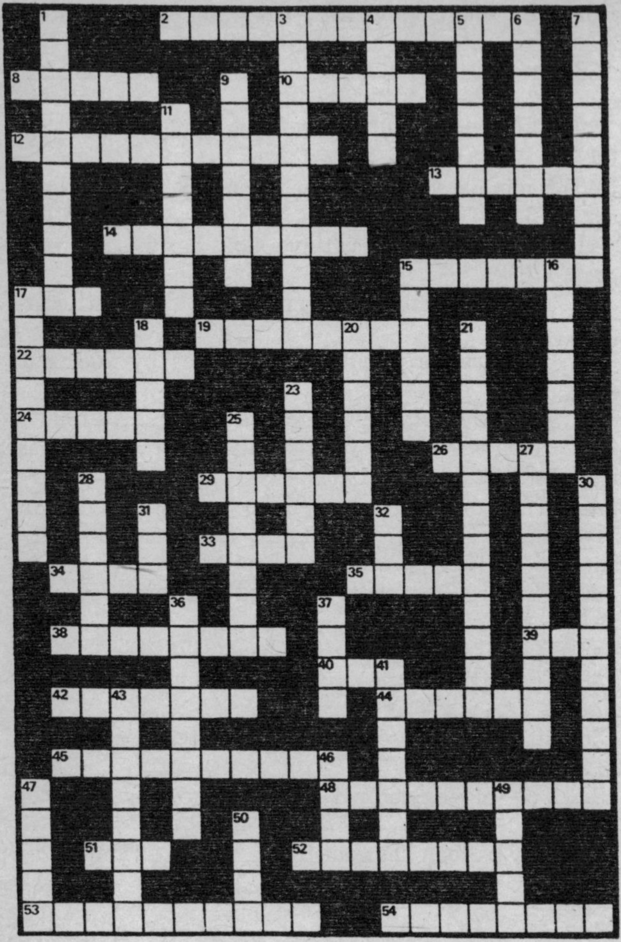

(Answers on page 128)

# CROSSWORD OF THE GREATEST

*Clues*

1. Largest prehistoric mammal, still existing in a smaller form. (48)
2. Heaviest prehistoric animal. (47)
3. Covers greatest area by a single clonal growth. (50)
4. Largest aquarium. (55)
5. Tallest species of tree. (50)
6. Longest river in Ireland. (63)
7. Allegedly killed 900 Japanese soldiers. (214)
8. Snake with the longest fangs. (39)
9. Largest grocery chain. (163)
10. Largest asteroid. (72)
11. Heaviest flying bird. (36)
12. Largest park (2 words). (54)
13. Largest lake in Great Britain. (65)
14. Largest atoll. (60)

15 across. Longest segmented worm in Britain. (45)

15 down. Largest aircraft manufacturer. (161)

16. Longest glacier. (66)

17 across. Has largest volcano crater on earth. (57)

17 down. Has largest wing span. (36)

18. Largest natural lake in Wales. (65)
19. Largest moon. (72)
20. Largest zoological preserve. (54)
21. Largest ship wrecked. (140)
22. Largest land carnivore in Britain. (29)
23. Grass as tall as a tree. (51)
24. Tallest tribe. (10)
25. British spider with the greatest leg span. (42)
26. Bat with the greatest wing span. (30)
27. Largest lake island in Great Britain. (60)
28. Largest desert. (65)
29. Largest peninsula. (60)
30. Largest concrete dam (2 words). (126)

31. Tallest cathedral spire. (211)
32. Longest lake in Great Britain, counting its three arms. (65)
33. Highest peak in the greatest mountain range. (63)
34. Largest leaf. (54)
35. Longest human bone. (17)
36. Heaviest wood. (52)
37. Theoretically the most abundant element in the earth. (56)
38. Largest monkey. (31)
39. Largest prehistoric bird. (48)
40. Weaver with the largest web. (42)
41. Largest inland island. (60)
42. Largest seed. (54)
43. Largest rodent. (31)
44. Wild animal with the longest horns. (32)
45. Longest recorded dinosaur. (47)
46. Has the most feathers. (37)
47. Longest snake in Britain. (39)
48. Largest lake in England. (65)
49. Largest frog now found in Britain. (40)
50. Largest ant in Britain. (44)
51. Longest river in Scotland. (63)
52. Biggest advertiser. (161)
53. Largest amphibian. (40)
54. Largest living land animal. (27)

(Answers on page 128)

# EASY-TO-HARD CRYPTOGRAMS

All the letters you need to read the messages are here (sometimes more than you need). If you can find the pattern by which the letters, groups of letters, and words were scrambled, and then unscramble them, you will discover the secret message.

1. LINER PASSENGER LARGEST THE WAS ELIZABETH QUEEN THE.
2. THETA LLEST INHAB ITEDB UILDI NGISS EARST OWER.
3. S DGLAS TAINE DESTS THEOL ALHAS THEDR URGCA AUGSB.
4. AEG BDI CRB DTS EEH FGI GHE HHT ISI JEG KRO LGL MAY NOR.
5. ALUCI BAZAR CATEW DASTH EELIG FHTES GTADU HLTHU IMAN.
6. SWEDE TSAHN HELAR OTSEG RECAR REIR.
7. TFEFC HERIH ELHVS ETAEW IOSIA FWANY.
8. AIHNN BLIAA FNHHC KITCI LHSTO GITGL.
9. HTRED EOR KCAMED HTS EOLE WTS APSSGAE.
10. SAYNR RAIIA HLAIS HHETN EALSA WGTRA EOSMT UANWI TTEER IHLWF EGEHL T. (There are two messages here.)

(Answers on pages 129–130)

(Answers on page 131)

# AROUND THE WORLD

Mr and Mrs Travers took a trip around the world. Upon their return, they spoke with enthusiasm about the many things they had seen and learned, but often they forgot to mention the name of the country they were talking about. From the clues below, can you tell what countries they visited? Enter the names into the proper blocks, and see if you can complete the round-the-world tour.

1. Has the highest extinct volcano. (57)
2. May have the world's largest man-made lake. (126–127)
3. The world's greatest archipelago. (60)
4. Has the lowest point in the Sahara Desert (former name). (65)
5. Has the world's largest residential palace. (118)
6. Has the world's presently most productive copper mine. (135)

7 across. Has the highest airport. (152)

7 down. Has the youngest king. (184)

8. Has the highest mortality rate from snakebite. (39)
9. Has the oldest educational institution. (209)

10 across. Has the narrowest navigable straits. (58)

10 down. Has the steepest standard gauge railway gradient by adhesion. (147)

11. Has the world's hottest town. (68)
12. Country of origin of the maidenhair (ginkgo) tree. (51)
13. Had the person with the highest income from royalties. (234)
14. Had the greatest ancient aqueduct. (125)
15. Has the largest maternity hospital. (183)

16 down. Shares the world's deepest cave. (61)

16 across. The greatest coffee-consuming country. (205)

17. Has the oldest castle. (117)

18. Had the worst inflation. (202)

19 down. Has the loneliest tree. (51)

19 across. Has the largest earthworks built prior to the mechanical era. (129)

20. Shares the world's deepest cave. (61)

21. Shares the largest delta. (64)

22. Has the tallest lighthouse. (131)

23. Had the flightless moa. (48)

24. Gave the most expensive banquet. (165)

25. Displays the largest merchant fleet. (205)

26. Has the tallest columns. (130)

27. Has the largest exposed rocky outcrop. (60)

28. Had the biggest accidental explosion. (214)

29. Has the most complicated clockwork. (158)

30. Shares the largest delta. (64)

## FIND THE BRACKET

None of the answers given to each question is exactly right. The right answer is in between two of the answers given (B, C, D); or it is smaller than the smallest answer given (A); or it is larger than the largest answer given (E).

1. The time it would take a metal weight, if dropped in the deepest part of the ocean, to reach the bottom: (58)

| | | | | | | | | |
|---|---|---|---|---|---|---|---|---|
| A | 5 minutes | B | 1 hour | C | 5 hours | D | 1 day | E |

2. The weight of the heaviest hailstones: (68)

| | | | | | | | | |
|---|---|---|---|---|---|---|---|---|
| A | 1½ lb. | B | 2 lb. | C | 3 lb. | D | 10 lb. | E |

3. Old Faithful, erupting on an average of every 66 minutes, may be off schedule by as much as: (57)

| | | | | | | | | |
|---|---|---|---|---|---|---|---|---|
| A | 1 minute | B | 5 minutes | C | 10 minutes | D | 15 minutes | E |

4. Encke's Comet, which has the shortest period known, returns every: (71)

A — 3 years — B — 5 years — C — 10 years — D — 15 years — E

5. The estimated number of meteorites reaching the earth's land surface each year: (69)

A — 200 — B — 2,000 — C — 2,000,000 — D — 2,000,000,000 — E

6. An ounce of gold could be stretched: (78)

A — 1 mile — B — 10 miles — C — 100 miles — D — 1,000 miles — E

7. The world's longest contested law suit lasted: (193)

A — 10 years — B — 100 years — C — 500 years — D — 1,000 years — E

8. The smallest full grown dog weighs: (34)

A — 8 oz. — B — 1 lb. — C — 2 lb. — D — 3 lb. — E

9. The wing span of the smallest butterfly: (45)

A — 1 in — B — 1½ in — C — 2 in — D — 2½ in — E

10. The largest European catfish weighed: (41)

A — 250 lb. — B — 500 lb. — C — 750 lb. — D — 1,000 lb. — E

11. The deepest roots of the wild fig tree: (50)

A — 100 ft — B — 200 ft — C — 300 ft — D — 500 ft — E

12. Marjorie Gestring won an Olympic gold medal at age: (309)

A — 12 yr — B — 14 yr — C — 16 yr — D — 18 yr — E

13. The highest speed of a swimmer: (321)

A — 3 m.p.h. — B — 5 m.p.h. — C — 7 m.p.h. — D — 9 m.p.h. — E

14. Gunnar Larsson won an Olympic 400m swim by: (323)

| A | | B | | C | | D | | E |
|---|---|---|---|---|---|---|---|---|
| | 1 in | | 1 ft | | 1 yard | | 100 yards | |

15. The estimated number of Picasso's works: (88)

| A | | B | | C | | D | | E |
|---|---|---|---|---|---|---|---|---|
| | 140 | | 1,400 | | 14,000 | | 140,000 | |

16. The time Tommy Seddon has spent so far in Coventry: (203)

| A | | B | | C | | D | | E |
|---|---|---|---|---|---|---|---|---|
| | 6 mo. | | 1 yr | | 2 yr | | 3 yr | |

17. The number of unexploded bombs Werner Stephan defused: (224)

| A | | B | | C | | D | | E |
|---|---|---|---|---|---|---|---|---|
| | 10 | | 100 | | 1,000 | | 10,000 | |

18. A quorum in the House of Lords: (185)

| A | | B | | C | | D | | E |
|---|---|---|---|---|---|---|---|---|
| | 5 | | 50 | | 100 | | 150 | |

19. The closest settlement to the South Pole: (116)

| A | | B | | C | | D | | E |
|---|---|---|---|---|---|---|---|---|
| | 10 yards | | 1,000 yards | | 10 miles | | 500 miles | |

20. The longest period of human unconsciousness: (20)

| A | | B | | C | | D | | E |
|---|---|---|---|---|---|---|---|---|
| | 5 yr | | 10 yr | | 20 yr | | 30 yr | |

21. The earliest operation with anaesthesia: (24)

| A | | B | | C | | D | | E |
|---|---|---|---|---|---|---|---|---|
| | 1750 | | 1800 | | 1850 | | 1900 | |

22. The longest bird migration: (37)

| A | | B | | C | | D | | E |
|---|---|---|---|---|---|---|---|---|
| | 1,000 miles | | 2,500 miles | | 5,000 miles | | 7,500 miles | |

23. The heaviest silver nugget, troy weight: (82)

| A | | B | | C | | D | | E |
|---|---|---|---|---|---|---|---|---|
| | 5 lb. | | 10 lb. | | 25 lb. | | 2,500 lb. | |

24. The number of rooms in Biltmore House: (120)

| 50 | 100 | 200 | 500 |
A B C D E

25. The number of corners to turn in the Targa Florio race: (304)

| 1,000 | 5,000 | 10,000 | 15,000 |
A B C D E

26. The age of the youngest Olympic winner: (309)

| 10 | 12 | 14 | 16 |
A B C D E

27. Damascus has been continuously inhabited since: (181)

| 3000 B.C. | 2000 B.C. | 1000 B.C. | A.D. 1 |
A B C D E

28. The oldest watch was made in: (159)

| 1400 | 1500 | 1600 | 1700 |
A B C D E

29. The time workers are allowed to climb the longest stairs in Britain: (132)

| 10 mins | 20 mins | 30 mins | 40 mins |
A B C D E

30. The greatest number of chin-ups: (287)

| 50 | 100 | 150 | 200 |
A B C D E

31. The greatest amount paid by a single cheque: (202)

| £1,000,000 | £10,000,000 | £100,000,000 | £1,000,000,000 |
A B C D E

32. The age of the youngest pope: (212)

| 15 | 30 | 45 | 60 |
A B C D E

33. The shortest time for making a suit, from sheep to man: (231)

| 1 hour | 5 hours | 1 day | 5 days |
A B C D E

34. The highest horse racing odds were ____ to 1: (279)

| A | | B | | C | | D | | E |
|---|---|---|---|---|---|---|---|---|
| \| | 100 | \| | 1,000 | \| | 10,000 | \| | 100,000 | \| |

35. The highest speed attained by any wheeled land vehicle: (141, 148)

| A | | B | | C | | D | | E |
|---|---|---|---|---|---|---|---|---|
| \| | Mach 1 | \| | Mach 2 | \| | Mach 3 | \| | Mach 4 | \| |

36. In the longest British trial spanning 827 days, the jury was out: (193)

| A | | B | | C | | D | | E |
|---|---|---|---|---|---|---|---|---|
| \| | 1 hour | \| | 1 day | \| | 1 week | \| | 1 month | \| |

37. The shortest war: (189)

| A | | B | | C | | D | | E |
|---|---|---|---|---|---|---|---|---|
| \| | 1 hour | \| | 1 day | \| | 1 week | \| | 1 month | \| |

38. The cost per hour for displaying the curtain across Rifle Gap: (169)

| A | | B | | C | | D | | E |
|---|---|---|---|---|---|---|---|---|
| \| | $100 | \| | $500 | \| | $1,000 | \| | $25,000 | \| |

39. The altitude record for model aircraft: (154)

| A | | B | | C | | D | | E |
|---|---|---|---|---|---|---|---|---|
| \| | 1,000 ft | \| | 5,000 ft | \| | 25,000 ft | \| | 100,000 ft | \| |

40. The age of the youngest solo pilot: (154)

| A | | B | | C | | D | | E |
|---|---|---|---|---|---|---|---|---|
| \| | 9 | \| | 11 | \| | 13 | \| | 15 | \| |

41. The most expensive airplane ride, per mile: (150)

| A | | B | | C | | D | | E |
|---|---|---|---|---|---|---|---|---|
| \| | $10 | \| | $50 | \| | $500 | \| | $50,000,000 | \| |

42. The number of umbrellas lost on the Japanese National Railways in 1970: (147)

| A | | B | | C | | D | | E |
|---|---|---|---|---|---|---|---|---|
| \| | 4,000 | \| | 40,000 | \| | 400,000 | \| | 4,000,000 | \| |

43. A bicycle is pictured in a stained glass window dated: (145)

| | | | | | | | | |
|---|---|---|---|---|---|---|---|---|
| A | 1600 | B | 1700 | C | 1800 | D | 1900 | E |

44. Date of the earliest mechanically-propelled passenger vehicle: (141)

| | | | | | | | | |
|---|---|---|---|---|---|---|---|---|
| A | 1750 | B | 1800 | C | 1850 | D | 1900 | E |

45. A Liberty ship was built in: (139)

| | | | | | | | | |
|---|---|---|---|---|---|---|---|---|
| A | 1 week | B | 2 weeks | C | 3 weeks | D | 4 weeks | E |

46. The largest production of gold per ton: (135)

| | | | | | | | | |
|---|---|---|---|---|---|---|---|---|
| A | 1 ounce | B | 8 ounces | C | 1 lb. | D | 5 lb. | E |

47. The diamonds extracted from 21,000,000 tons of earth: (135)

| | | | | | | | | |
|---|---|---|---|---|---|---|---|---|
| A | 1 ton | B | 5 tons | C | 10 tons | D | 100 tons | E |

48. The greatest distance ever covered by a ship in one day, in nautical miles: (136)

| | | | | | | | | |
|---|---|---|---|---|---|---|---|---|
| A | 250 | B | 500 | C | 750 | D | 1,000 | E |

49. The lowest birth weight for a surviving infant: (17)

| | | | | | | | | |
|---|---|---|---|---|---|---|---|---|
| A | 8 ounce | B | 12 ounces | C | 1 lb. | D | 2 lb. | E |

50. The most pairs of legs on a centipede: (45)

| | | | | | | | | |
|---|---|---|---|---|---|---|---|---|
| A | 50 | B | 100 | C | 150 | D | 200 | E |

(Answers on page 131)

# SHORT REBUSES

Each illustration suggests a word. Write the letters of the first word, then add the letters for words preceded by a plus sign. If there is a minus sign, those letters are to be crossed out from your sequence. When crossing out letters, some judgment must be exercised, as there may be a choice available. No homonyms are used; thus, the picture of an eye would stand for the letters EYE. (Answers on page 132.)

1. Don ______ is the tallest living person. (8)

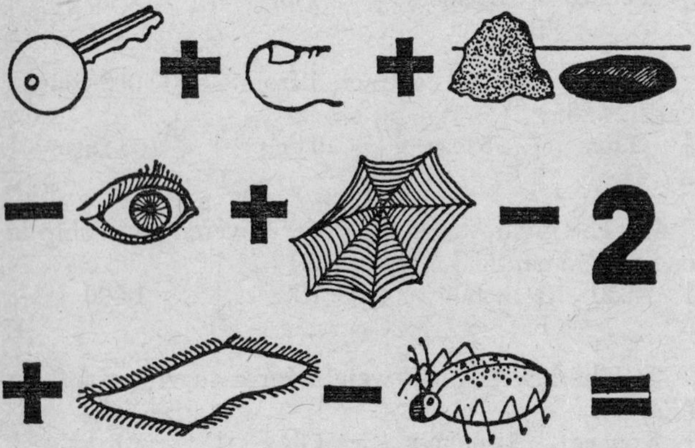

2. Jane ______ was the tallest woman in medical history. (8)

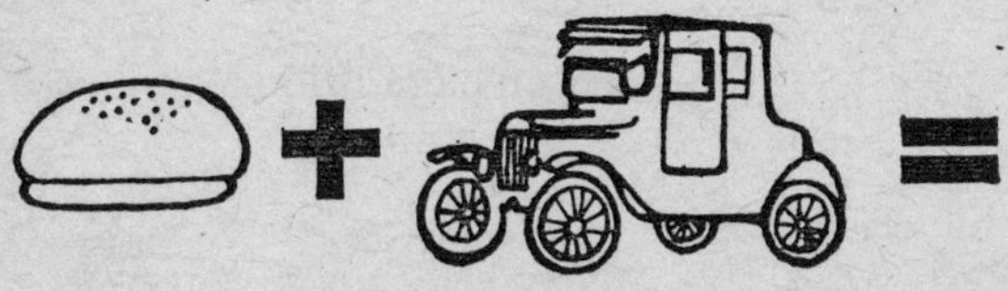

3. Hopkins ______ weighed 13 lb. at the age of 16. (10)

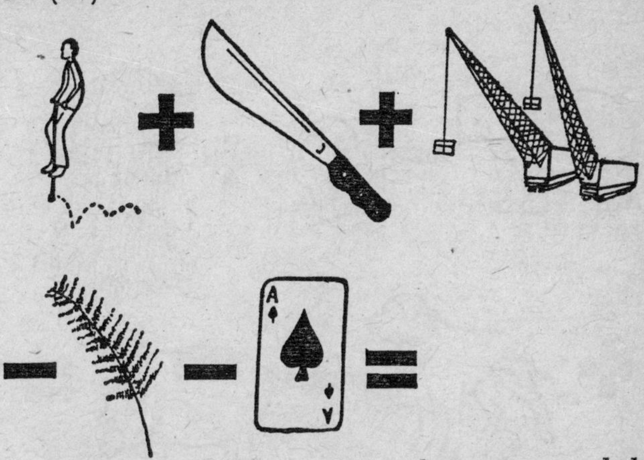

4. William ______ was the heaviest recorded British man. (11)

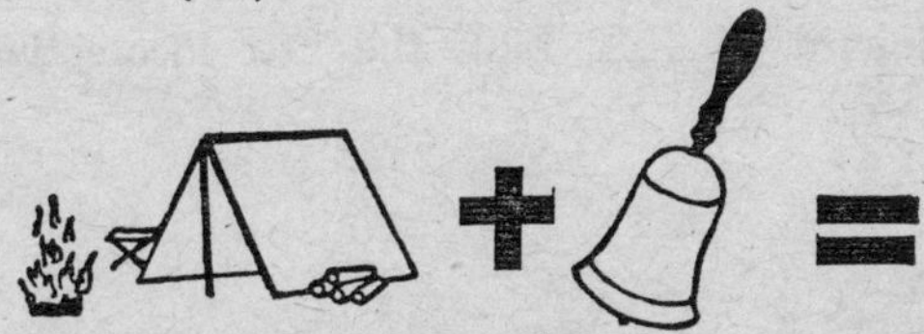

5. Nellie ______ was the heaviest recorded British woman. (11)

6. John ______ gave the earliest public demonstration of television. (109)

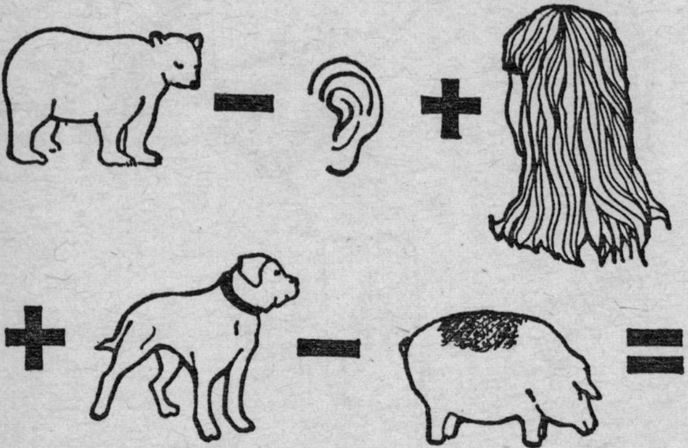

7. Richard ______ built the first locomotive on rails. (145)

8. Nathaniel ______ was the first to sight the Antarctica continent. (218–219)

9. John ______ and son Clifford walked from Halifax to Vancouver. (221)

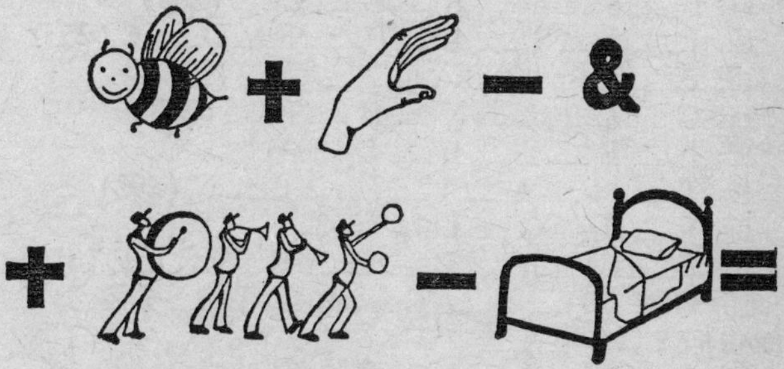

10. Eleven-year-old Becky ______ cycled across the United States. (221)

# SPORTS AND GAMES PERSONALITIES

Fill in the missing letters, and you will have the name of a person or animal famous in sports or games. Then identify the sport or game.

1. A __ I __ E __ E __ H (245)
2. D __ W __ F __ A __ E __ (323)
3. J __ M __ I __ E (266)
4. A __ T __ U __ W __ I __ F __ R __ (287)
5. E __ M __ N __ H __ L __ A __ Y (306)
6. P __ T __ R __ P __ O __ I __ (247)
7. G __ R __ I __ L __ S __ B __ R __ (257)
8. T __ D __ R __ K __ (269)
9. C __ A __ L __ T __ E __ O __ (299)
10. M __ C __ A __ L __ U __ L (330)
11. R __ S __ C __ E __ E __ L __ (250)
12. J __ N __ T __ A __ P __ N __ O __ E (255)
13. P __ T __ I __ K __ E __ C __ (263)
14. G __ L __ I __ N __ H __ E __ (268)
15. B __ B __ Y __ U __ L (293)
16. T __ M __ A __ I __ U __ T __ N (282)
17. J __ H __ C __ B __ (303)
18. S __ U __ R __ M __ C __ E __ Z __ E (316)
19. G __ O __ F __ E __ L __ D __ I __ R __ (249)
20. J __ C __ H __ L __ E __ (262)
21. M __ C __ T __ E __ I __ L __ R (286)
22. J __ M __ E __ M __ N (301)
23. T __ L __ A __ (291)
24. P __ A __ O __ U __ M __ (327)
25. R __ X __ M __ R __ U __ (296)
26. D __ V __ D __ A __ K __ N __ (275)
27. W __ L __ E __ L __ N __ R __ M (248)
28. H __ A __ H __ R __ L __ O __ (266)
29. P __ T __ I __ I __ T __ P __ E __ (295)
30. P __ U __ W __ T __ E __ S (311)

(Answers on pages 132–133)

# INCONGRUOUS MEMBERS

Find which term in each set does not belong there.

1. A. Number of persons whose native tongue is Manx, in 1974. (90)
   B. Number of pounds Alfred Nobel bequeathed to his wife. (238)
   C. Number of performances of *As You Like It* at the Shaftesbury Theatre. (105)
   D. The closest in millions of miles that a comet has come to the earth. (71)
2. A. Martin Lindsay.
   B. Arthur Godfrey.
   C. Andrew Croft.
   D. 49 dogs.
   E. 73 cats. (219)
3. A. Riding.
   B. Fencing.
   C. Shooting.
   D. Long jump.
   E. Swimming (300 metres).
   F. Running (cross-country). (300)
4. A. Sea snake. (39)
   B. Stonefish. (42)
   C. Black widow. (43)
   D. Python. (39)
   E. Death cap toadstool. (54)
   F. Box jelly. (46)
5. A. Grand Coulee Dam.
   B. Fort Peck Dam.
   C. Grande Dixence.
   D. Ingurskaya Dam.
   E. Wilson Dam. (126)
6. A. Verrazano-Narrows Bridge.
   B. Mackinac Straits Bridge.
   C. Firth of Forth Road Bridge.
   D. Pont de Québec.
   E. Royal Gorge Bridge. (123–124)

7. A. Pyramids of Giza.
   B. Temple of Artemis.
   C. Tomb of King Mausolus.
   D. Parthenon.
   E. Hanging Gardens of Semiramis.
   F. Statue of Zeus.
   G. Colossus of Rhodes.
   H. Lighthouse of Alexandria. (128)
8. A. *United States.*
   B. *Queen Mary.*
   C. *Nautilus.*
   D. *Lusitania.*
   E. *Bismarck.* (136–137)
9. A. Bust of Abraham Lincoln.
   B. Bust of Dwight Eisenhower.
   C. Bust of Gerald Ford. (81)
10. A. Ulysses S. Grant.
    B. Robert E. Lee.
    C. Stonewall Jackson.
    D. Jefferson Davis. (89)
11. A. I Hsing.
    B. Liang Ling-tsan.
    C. Rex Harrison. (158)
12. Railways in (A) India, (B) Pakistan, (C) Ceylon, (D) Britain, (E) Spain, (F) Portugal, (G) Argentina, and (H) Chile. (146)
13. A. Ellis.
    B. Diable.
    C. Royale.
    D. St. Joseph. (199)
14. A. Physics.
    B. Chemistry.
    C. Philosophy.
    D. Medicine and Physiology.
    E. Literature.
    F. Peace.
    G. Economics. (238)

15. A. 3 lb. piece of metal.
    B. 26 keys.
    C. 3 sets of rosary beads.
    D. 16 religious medals.
    E. 1 bracelet.
    F. 1 necklace.
    G. 3 pairs of tweezers.
    H. 4 nail clippers.
    I. 17 fish hooks.
    J. 39 nail files.
    K. 3 metal chains.
    L. 88 coins. (21)
16. A. Neil Armstrong.
    B. Thomas Stafford.
    C. Eugene Cernan.
    D. John Young. (215)
17. A. Yancos.
    B. Temiar.
    C. Aimores. (84)

(Answers on pages 133–134)

# THREE-TO-THREE MAZE

Find the *shortest* route from the top 3 to the bottom 3. Then tell the significance of the number you have found. (84)

(Answer on page 134)

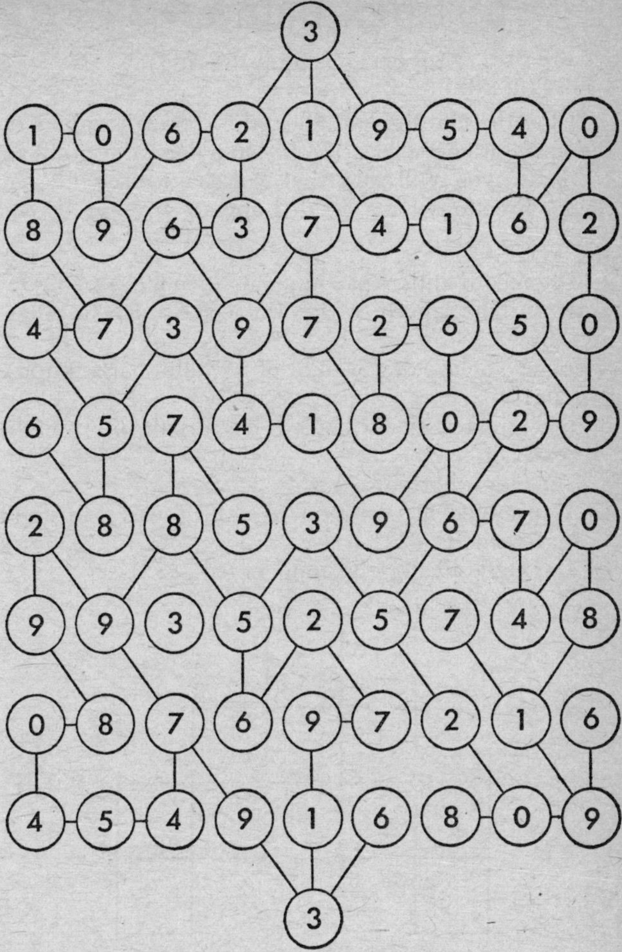

# TEN DIGITS

(Answers on pages 134–135)

Using the clues given, fill in the proper numbers in the appropriate blocks. If you have done the problem correctly, you will find that you have used all ten digits. Fractions have been dropped.

I.

1. The record antler span of a moose, in inches. (32)
2 across. The length of the Malacca Straits, in miles. (58)
2 down. The greatest weight of a whale shark, in tons. (40)
3. The greatest load hauled by a pair of draught horses, in tons. (33)
4. The oldest horse. (33)
5. A sustained acceleration of _____g was withstood for 5 seconds. (22)
6. The highest kangaroo jump, in feet. (33)

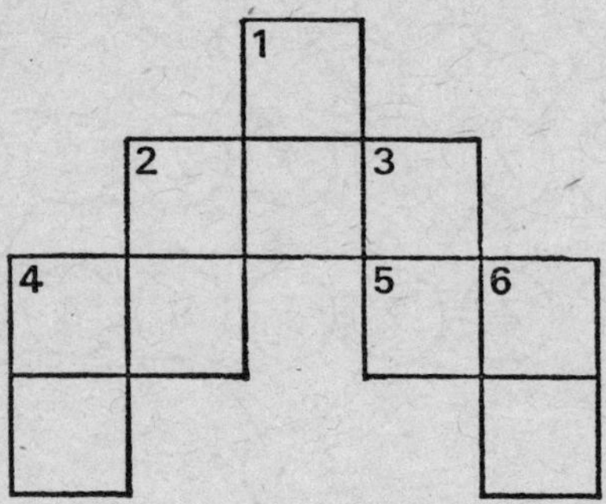

II.

1. Height of the Yerba Buena Island tunnel, in feet. (128)

2 across. The weight of Sputnik I, in pounds. (75)

2 down. Longest seaweed, in feet. (50)

3. Weight of the heaviest gold nugget, in pounds. (82)
4. Seating capacity of the smallest regularly operated professional theatre in the United Kingdom. (104)
5. The longest lightning flash, in miles. (67)

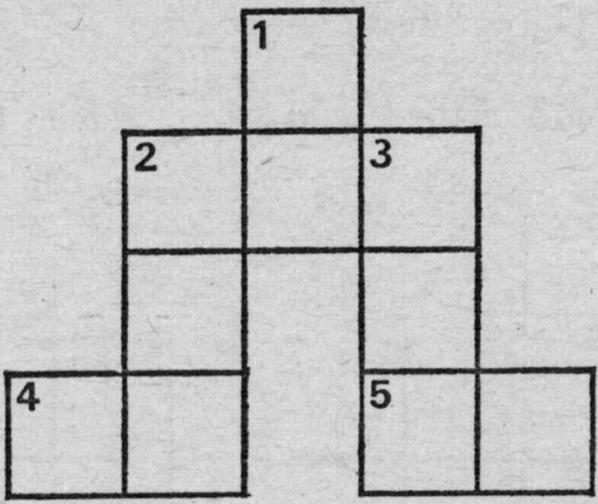


III.

1 across. Weight of the largest carillon, in tons. (103)

1 down. GTV of Melbourne covered the Apollo XI moon mission for ____ continuous hours. (110)

2. A giant jellyfish had a tentacular span of ____ feet. (25)
3. The prehistoric Wansdyke earthwork ran ____ miles. (129)
4. Height of the tallest aspidistra, in inches. (50)
5. The record for rapid tunnelling is ____ feet in one day. (128)

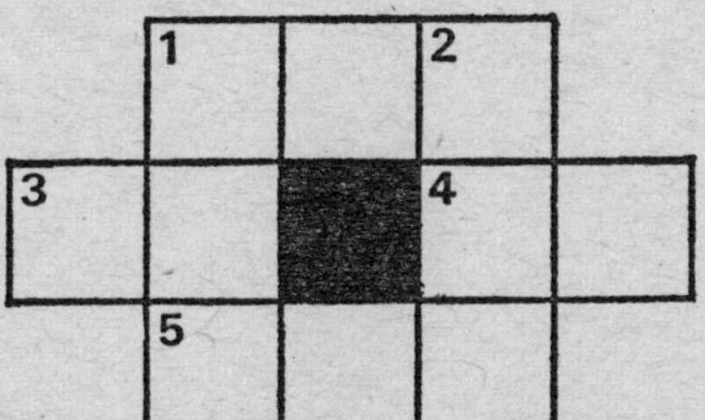

IV.

1. The world's most powerful piston engine car has _____ spark plugs. (142)
2. H.M.S. *Inflexible* carried armour _____ inches thick. (138)
3. Cleopatra's Needle is _____ feet tall. (130)
4. The longest animal horn measured is _____ inches. (32)

5 across. Hadrian's Wall ran _____ miles. (132)

5 down. The greatest live turkey weighed _____ pounds. (37)

6. The length of the *France* is _____ feet. (137)

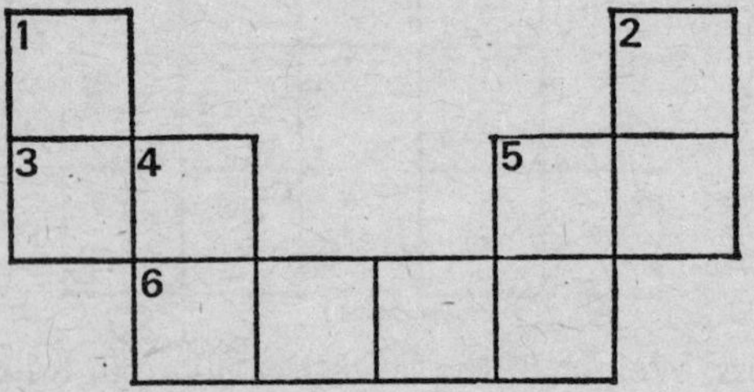

# ANAGRAMS

Unscramble the words on each line, then answer the question at the end of the set. Each word has been scrambled separately.

I. The Long Way Home
1. YWLIE STOP.
2. GLEEN GLON.
3. ANJU STASNEBIO.
4. HUJOSA MOUSCL.
5. HOJN ZLWGUELZ.
6. REWADD CHABE.
7. BRION KXON-THOJSONN.
8. RIYYU RAAGING.

Each of these men did the same thing, but in a different way. What records did they set? (149, 217, 218)

II. Fuzzy Menaces
1. CLAKB DOWWI.
2. NULFEN BWE.
3. OYKJEC.
4. TNOBTU.
5. RODAPOAD.
6. NOWRB CUSLERE.

What have each of these names in common? (43)

III. A Royal Shindig
1. ULIAQ SGEG.
2. ARNNIAI ARVICA.
3. CHISYARF SLAIT.
4. ASTOR BALM.
5. ROTAS KCAEPOC.
6. IFEO SRAG.
7. GFI GINRS.

8. REPYRSABR TWESE PEMHGACAN RETHBES.
9. SINEW.

Where did all these items appear? (165)

IV. An Exclusive Club

1. AJNE ULAP YTGET.
2. HJNO RUTHCRAMA.
3. DROHNSOLA L. NUTH.
4. LENIAD IWDGUL.
5. ONHJ D. LOREKFCRELE.
6. DRAWHO HESHGU.
7. YHREN DROF.
8. WARDEN ENMOLL.
9. H. SORS TROPE.

Tell what these men had in common. (233–234)

(Answers on pages 136–137)

## PLACES TO HIDE

Where might you go to try to avoid the perils of . . .

1. Income tax, but stay in Great Britain? (200)
2. Noise? (85)
3. Yellow fever, cholera nostras, and bubonic plague? (19)
4. Laughing sickness? (19)
5. Drought? (68)
6. Heavy air? (181)
7. The sea? (60)
8. Infant mortality? (182)
9. Premature death (males)? (182)
10. Premature death (females)? (182)
11. A shortage of doctors? (183)
12. A shortage of psychiatrists? (183)

13. Nuclear war? (192)
14. Murder? (196)
15. Suicide? (196)
16. Capital punishment? (197)
17. Starvation? (203)
18. Railways, but on mainland Great Britain? (205)
19. Altitude sickness? (61)
20. School? (209)
21. Wealth? (234)
22. Earthquake? (57)
23. Poverty? (340)
24. Inflation? (340)
25. Freezing, but in the British Isles? (67)

(Answers on pages 137–138)

## OPPOSITES

Tell in what way the two parts of each number are opposites.

1. O. (19)
   AB. (19)
2. D. (63)
   Nile. (63)
3. *France*. (137)
   *France II*. (140)
4. Dhaulagri, Himalayas. (152)
   El Lisan. (152)
5. British Petroleum. (160)
   British Olivetti. (161)
6. The Mexico and United States border. (179)
   The China and U.S.S.R. border. (179)
7. Dikson, U.S.S.R. (181)
   Puerto Williams, Chile. (181)
8. Reykjavik. (181)
   Wellington. (181)
9. Banks in Brazil. (201)
   Banks in Morocco. (201)

10. New York Harbor. (205)
Rotterdam-Europoort. (205)
11. The Hiroshima atom bomb. (192)
The Jamaican table tennis champion in 1958. (241)
12. Coleridge F.C. (273)
Tongham Youth Club and Hawley. (273)
13. Spanish, Venetian and Papal forces. (190)
Turkish forces. (190)
14. Statue of Liberty.
Motherland. (130)
15. The value of *Mona Lisa.* (87)
The value of *Mona Lisa.* (87)
16. Xenon. (77)
Hydrogen. (77)
17. Ubyx. (90)
Rotokas. (90)
18. Gertrude Ederle. (324)
Florence Chadwick. (324)
19. Talkers in Monaco. (207)
Talkers in Upper Volta. (207)
20. Diners in Uruguay. (204)
Diners in Sri Lanka. (204)

(Answers on page 138)

## DOUBLE ANSWERS

Each problem has two parts, but both parts have a similar answer. The words may have a slightly different spelling or pronunciation, or represent only part of a name or title.

1. The most famous female conjoined twins *and* the hotel with the most expensive suites in Britain. (16, 119)

2. A person who studied ancient Greek at age three *and* the Dijkpolder. (18, 131)

3. The largest coelenterate in British waters *and* a famous Sherlock Holmes story. (46)

4. The place where the highest surface wind was recorded *and* the monument that was once the tallest structure in the world. (68, 122)

5. The deepest crater on the moon *and* the largest reflector telescope in the British Isles. (70, 82)

6. The earliest known figurines *and* the hottest planet. (89, 72)

7. The largest building in ground area *and* the largest building in Britain. (115, 116)

8. Owner of the largest house in Ireland *and* the largest brewery in Europe. (120, 162)

9. The largest ballroom in the United Kingdom *and* Britain's rare *Epipogium aphyllum.* (120, 49)

10. The largest amusement resort *and* the winner of the most Oscars. (120, 108)

11. A feature of some modern football stadiums, *but* the largest will be found at the Imperial Palace. (120, 119)

12. Site of the Great Exhibition of 1851 *and* precious material weighing up to 70 tons. (121, 81)

13. The largest public house in the United Kingdom *and* a bird sometimes credited with the greatest all up weight. (121, 36)

14. At one time the largest liner *and* the largest artificial reservoir in the United Kingdom. (137, 127)

15. The tallest active geyser *and* Jouffroy d'Abbans's invention. (57, 136)

16. The largest vat in the United Kingdom *and* the first moon-landing mission. (132, 215)

17. Site of the earliest known mines in England *and* the M.P. with the longest span of service. (134, 187)

18. A star 26 times as bright as the sun *and* the first ship to cross the Atlantic under continuous steam power. (73, 136)

19. A sport whose first champion was J. A. Miskey *and* site of the first atomic pile. (320, 155)

20. The highest Bank of England notes *and* a famous story by Mark Twain. (202)

21. The largest vessel ever salvaged *and* the greatest invasion. (220, 189)

22. The earliest flying trapeze artist *and* a tight-fitting garment. (233)

23. The highest paid concert pianist *and* the first Prime Minister of Poland after World War I. (102)

24. The devices on which William Congreve specialised *and* the longest chorus line. (74, 105)

25. Probably the oldest recorded citizen of the United Kingdom *and* an author famous for treasure hunting. (14)

26. The greatest seller of any gramophone record *and* what London has experienced seven times this century. (107, 67)

(Answers on page 139)

## A SECRET MESSAGE

Before you can get the secret message, you have to match each clue in the numbered list to the correct name.

1. Shortest mature human in Britain. (10)
2. His hat brought the highest price. (170)
3. Achieved the first supersonic flight. (148)
4. Had lowest birth weight for a surviving infant. (17)
5. Achieved most knock-outs. (252)
6. Owned the earliest London theatre. (104)
7. His album led the U.S. long-player charts for 490 weeks. (107)
8. Her books have sold over 300,000,000 copies. (96)
9. A seat for her concert might cost $653. (102)
10. Launched first liquid-fuelled rocket. (75)
11. Achieved highest speed on land for a wheeled vehicle. (215)

12. Had first classical album to sell a million. (107)
13. Tallest basketball player. (247)
14. Had earliest recorded piece that eventually reached a million copies. (106)
15. Driver with the most world driving championships. (305)
16. Fastest builder of ships. (139)

A. Emili Rached
B. Charles Yeager
C. Juan-Manuel Fangio y Cia
D. Robert Goddard
E. Gary Gabelich
F. Agatha Christie
G. Marion Chapman
H. Napoleon
I. Archie Moore
J. Joyce Carpenter
K. Henry Kaiser
L. Van Cliburn
M. Johnny Mathis
N. Enrico Caruso
O. James Burbage
P. Johanna Lind

Now, to read the message hidden here, first put the names in numerical order. Note that every name has at least one A in it. What you want is the *second* letter after the *first* A.

Begin with the A in the name you have designated #1, and write down, in the space provided, the second letter following. Take the A in the name you have designated #2, and write down the second letter following it. Continue with all 16 names.

1 2 3 4 5 6 7 8 9 10 11 12 13 14 15 16
Second letter following A:

— — — — — — — — — — — — — — — —

(Answers on page 140)

# MARK'S MAZE

(Answers on page 140)

On the list below, put a check mark in front of each item if you believe the correct answer is more than 100:

A. The highest measured speed for a cricket ball bowled by any bowler, in m.p.h. (259)
B. Age of the oldest ever active judge. (195)
C. Height of the highest measured wave, in feet. (58)
D. Number of young a mother wild rabbit might have in a year. (36)
E. Weight in pounds of the largest pumpkin. (53)
F. The highest temperature in the British Isles, in degree F. (68)
G. Diameter in inches of the largest refracting telescope. (82)
H. Age of the midget Count Boruwalaski. (9)
I. Weight in pounds of the heaviest meteorite known to have fallen on the British Isles since 1623. (70)
J. Of the world's 109 tallest peaks, how many are in the Himalaya-Karakoram range? (63)
K. Number of irregular verbs in English. (90)
L. Fastest number of wing beats per second. (37)
M. Most hours spent deprived of all sensory stimulation. (22)
N. Height in feet of the tallest stalagmite. (61)
O. Number of days of the longest group hunger strike. (21)

Now prove your answers by entering the maze. When you come to a lettered door, see if you have checked that letter on your list. If so, pass through the lettered door. If not, by-pass it.

If you pass through the maze without hitting a dead end, you must be very knowledgeable. There is only one chance in 32,768 of accomplishing this feat entirely by chance. Going through the maze first is not fair!

# TRUTH OR CONSEQUENCES

A couple are chosen, and a question is asked of one of them. If the person does not answer correctly, he must perform one of the consequences. If he does answer correctly, his partner must perform it. Consequences should be chosen that are suitable to the contestant. After he has succeeded or failed, other persons in the group may want to try the same stunt.

1. Is the world's biggest aeroplane longer than it is wide? (149)
2. Which brought the higher price at an auction, a Ming bottle, or the Duke of Wellington's watch? (168, 159)
3. Which is larger, the largest tapestry or the largest embroidery? (171)
4. Which is larger, the largest flag or the largest table cloth? (170, 171)
5. Is Nauru north or south of the equator? (179)
6. In Washington, D.C., are there more telephones or people? (207)
7. Who was Prime Minister longer, Asquith or Churchill? (188)
8. Who reigned longer, Louis XIV or Queen Victoria? (183, 184)
9. Do more people immigate to or emigrate from the United Kingdom? (182)
10. Which should win a straight ¼-mile race, a greyhound or a horse? (34, 292)
11. Which is the greater, the Gulf Stream or the Antarctic Circumpolar Current? (59)
12. Which has the higher temperature, lightning or the surface of the sun? (67)
13. Is the Gateway Arch higher or broader? (129)
14. Which is larger, an indoor cucumber or an outdoor cucumber? (53)
15. Which is faster, a typist or a morse code operator? (232, 228)

16. Does the American Telephone and Telegraph Company have more employees or more shareholders? (160)

17. Did the United States Steel Corporation reach $1 billion first in sales or in assets? (160)

18. Who won the Battle of Towton, the white rose or the red rose? (189)

19. Are taxes higher in France or the United Kingdom? (200)

20. Which is older, the oldest parliament or the oldest national flag? (185, 170)

21. Where have more people walked, on the moon or on top of Mount Everest? (76, 307)

22. Which is larger, the moon or Mercury? (70, 71)

(Answers on page 140)

## Consequences

1. Try to remain completely motionless for five minutes, record 4½ hr. (21)

2. Recite Hamlet's soliloquy (Act III, Scene 1) as fast as possible, record 36 sec. (24)

3. Make as long an apple peeling as possible, record over 130 ft. (222)

4. Balance on one foot for five minutes, record 7½ hours. (223)

5. Stand a large coin on edge, and stack as many coins as possible on top, record 126. (224)

6. Pile 10p pieces on the back of the forearm, flip them up, and catch as many as possible, record 39. (224)

7. Make as many dancing taps as possible in a minute, record 1,440. (225)

8. Catch a fresh hen's egg, thrown by your partner, from as far a distance as possible without breaking it, record over 316 ft. (226)

9. Throw a Frisbee, record 285 ft. (226)

10. Knit as fast as possible for a minute, record 108 stitches. (228)

11. Thread as many needles as possible in two minutes, record average 63. (228)

12. Toss a paper aircraft, record 1,126 yds. (228)

13. Spin plates simultaneously, record 44. (229)

14. Throw a rope quoit, record 4,002 consecutive pegs. (229)

15. Throw a rolling pin, record over 144 ft. (230)

16. Skip a rope for one minute, record 286 turns. (230)

17. Spin a clock balance wheel, record over 5 min. (230)

18. Oscillate a yo-yo for one minute, record average over 67. (233)

19. Construct a house of cards, record 34 storeys. (227)

20. Toss a pancake for one minute, record average 77. (228)

21. Throw a gum boot, record over 119 ft. (226)

22. Bale a quart of water with a thimble, record average under two minutes. (229)

# MATHEMATICAL TRUE OR FALSE

In each group, some of the statements are true, some false. Place the number given in either the true or false column. If you have done this correctly, the totals of the two columns will be the same.

| | True | False |
|---|---|---|
| 1. A. The longest stalactite is 157 feet. (61) | ____ | ____ |
| B. The greatest number of rounds in a prize fight is 278. (250) | ____ | ____ |
| C. The Colossus of Rhodes was 117 feet tall. (128) | ____ | ____ |
| D. The base line of the Great Pyramid is 109 feet. (128) | ____ | ____ |
| E. The most knockdowns in a world title prize fight is 14. (251) | ____ | ____ |
| F. The lowest recorded temperature in the atmosphere is —143°C. (67) | ____ | ____ |
| TOTALS | ____ | ____ |

| | True | False |
|---|---|---|
| 2. A. The most moves in a tournament chess game is 315. (255) | ____ | ____ |
| B. The longest straight hole-in-one is 689 yards. (285) | ____ | ____ |
| C. The combined weight of the heaviest twins is 1300 lb. (11) | ____ | ____ |
| D. A vole may have 611 young in a year. (31) | ____ | ____ |
| E. The oldest tortoise may live 105 years. (25) | ____ | ____ |
| F. A mother cat has had a total of 420 kittens. (35) | ____ | ____ |
| TOTALS | ____ | ____ |

| | | True | False |
|---|---|---|---|
| 3. A. | The tallest tree in Britain is 265 feet. (51) | ___ | ___ |
| B. | The jet stream has been recorded at 408 m.p.h. (67) | ___ | ___ |
| C. | The greatest temperature change in a day is 65°F. (67) | ___ | ___ |
| D. | The highest room in Carlsbad Caverns is 143 feet. (61) | ___ | ___ |
| E. | A library book has been returned 300 years after due. (98) | ___ | ___ |
| F. | Sandringham House has 365 rooms. (120) | ___ | ___ |
| | TOTALS | ___ | ___ |

(Answers on page 141)

## SEESAW

Identify the pictures, and then decide which end of the seesaw should go down. Imagine the largest specimen known of the particular kind illustrated.

| | | | |
|---|---|---|---|
| 1. | (Quetzalcóatl) (128) | △ | (Great Pyramid) (128) |
| 2. | (Heaviest man) (11) | △ | (Pig) (173) |
| 3. | (Cake) (204) | △ | (Elephant) (27) |
| 4. | (Polar bear) (29) | △ | (Tiger) (29) |
| 5. | (St. Bernard) (33) | △ | (Ostrich) (36) |

6. (Gorilla) (Giant clam)
(30) △ (46)

7. (Chicken) (Rabbit)
(37) △ (36)

8. (Bee hummingbird) (Sphinx moth)
(36) △ (36)

9. (Blue whale) (Aeroplane)
(25) △ (149)

10. (Cut diamond) (Spider)
(81) △ (42)

11. (Car) (Kite)
(142) △ (228)

12. (Brachiosaurus) (Bulldozer)
(47) △ (143)

13. (Cabbage) (Cauliflower)
(53) △ (53)

14. (Pearl) (Potato)
(81) △ (53)

15. (Shark) (String ball)
(40) △ (231)

(Answers on page 141)

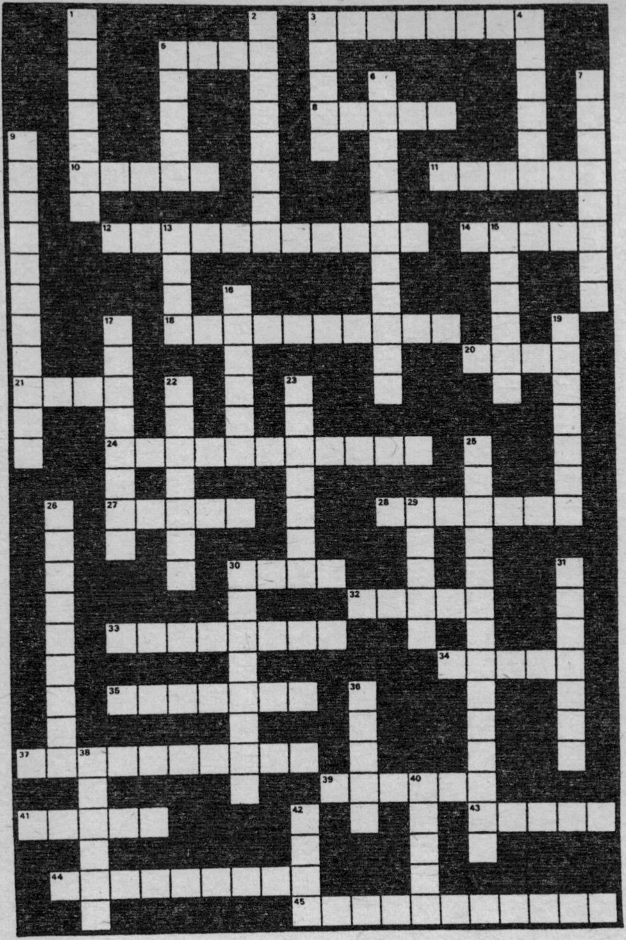

# CROSSWORD OF THE SMALLEST

*Clues*

1. Lightest metal. (78)
2. Lightest element. (77)
3 across. Smallest monkey. (31)
3 down. Smallest pygmies. (10)
4. Shortest snake. (39)
5 across. Shortest fish. (41)
5 down. Smallest lizard. (38)
6. Smallest bird. (36)
7. Smallest flowering plant. (52)
8. Professional name of the most famous midget. (9)
9. Lightest heavyweight champion. (250)
10. Smallest church. (211)
11. Lightest antelope. (32)
12. Narrowest street (3 words). (206)
13. Smallest coin. (202)
14. Smallest rodent. (31)
15. Smallest seed. (54)
16. Smallest human bone. (17)
17. Smallest pony. (33)
18. Least populated territories. (180)
19. Smallest starfish in British waters. (42)
20. Smallest marketed camera. (83)
21. Shortest known tribe. (10)
22. Smallest major planet. (71)
23. Smallest newt. (40)
24. Smallest book with metal type (2 words). (95)
25. Smallest "state" having some diplomatic privileges (3 words). (179)
26. Smallest crustacean (2 words). (43)
27. Smallest republic. (179)
28. Smallest independent country. (179)
29. Lowest value coin. (202)
30 across. Smallest true deer. (32)
30 down. Smallest colony. (179)

31. Smallest cathedral in the United Kingdom (2 words). (210)

32. Smallest tree frog. (40)

33. Smallest totally marine mammal (2 words). (28)

34. Least populous of the new Welsh counties. (180)

35. Smallest aeroplane flown. (150)

36. Smallest spider in Britain. (42)

37. Smallest nature reserve. (54)

38. Smallest moon in the solar system. (72)

39. Smallest living carnivore. (29)

40. Name of smallest trans-Atlantic boat (2 words). (219)

41. Smallest ant. (44)

42. Queen regnant with the shortest reign. (184)

43. Country with lowest death rate. (182)

44. Was the smallest district in Northern Ireland (2 words). (180)

45. Country with the lowest rate of natural increase (2 words). (182)

(Answers on page 142)

## MULTIPLE CHOICE SHIP

Choose the answer to the question which seems correct, and circle the letter which precedes the answer.

1. What Mary Mallon gave to 1,300 people, for which she was much criticised: (19)

   C. Payments on bad cheques
   L. Forged tickets to Wimbledon
   F. Bouquets of ragweed
   N. Typhoid fever

2. The play with the longest Broadway run is: (105)
   I. *Fiddler on the Roof*
   A. *West Side Story*
   E. *My Fair Lady*
   R. *Carousel*

3. The largest opera house is: (103)
   I. Cow Palace
   M. Lincoln Center
   A. Teatro della Scala
   L. Bolshoi Theatre

4. The singer who has made the most recordings is: (107)
   D. Bing Crosby
   V. Elvis Presley
   I. Lata Mangeshker
   E. The Beatles (separate and group)

5. The largest palace is: (118)
   E. Vatican Palace
   T. Imperial Palace
   N. Buckingham Palace
   I. The Citadel

6. The stadium which holds the most spectators is: (120)
   N. Maracanã Municipal Stadium
   D. Empire Stadium
   Z. Strahov Stadium
   R. Azteca Stadium

If you have circled all the correct letters, you will spell out the name of a ship. Identify the type of ship and tell why it is famous. (138)

(Answer on page 142)

# MULTIPLE CHOICE INSECT

Choose the answer to the question which seems correct, and circle the letter which precedes the answer.

1. The largest egg is laid by the: (26)
   C. Whale shark
   S. Golden eagle
   M. Ostrich
   B. Python

2. The largest stained glass window will be found at: (212)
   A. The Vatican
   P. Reims
   O. St. Paul's Cathedral
   I. John F. Kennedy International Airport

3. The creature with the largest eye is the: (26)
   N. Whale
   C. Giant squid
   I. Giraffe
   T. Horse

4. The hardest contagious disease to catch is: (19)
   T. Tuberculosis
   A. Leprosy
   D. Measles
   F. Dandruff

5. Anatole France, the famous French writer, was also known for his: (18)
   L. Low shoes
   I. Diamond stickpin
   D. Small brain
   E. First wristwatch

6. The longest animal ever recorded is the: (25)
   A. Giant jellyfish
   S. Boa constrictor

R. Brontosaurus
Y. Sea serpent

Now, if you have circled all the correct letters, they will spell out the name of an insect. Tell what record this insect holds. (44)

(Answer on page 142)

## MULTIPLE CHOICE ATHLETE

Choose the answer to the question which seems correct, and circle the letter which precedes the answer.

1. The tallest statue is: (130)
   B. Christ of the Andes
   N. Motherland
   W. Abraham Lincoln
   R. Colossus of Rhodes

2. The most abundant bird is the: (36)
   A. Chicken
   H. Sparrow
   O. Starling
   I. Quelea

3. The most expensive land is found in: (166)
   M. New York
   I. Hong Kong
   C. London
   B. Tokyo

4. The most popular Kennel Club dog is the: (34)
   K. Alsatian
   B. Cocker spaniel
   T. Poodle
   I. Beagle

5. The most valuable fur is: (33)
R. Mink
F. Chinchilla
L. Sea otter
N. Silver fox

6. The first day R. H. Macy's opened for business, the total sales amounted to: (165)
A. $11.06
I. $110.60
O. $1106.06
S. $11,060.06

7. The biggest explosion ever witnessed by man was: (73)
C. Nagasaki
U. Crab Nebula
R. Krakatoa
O. Vesuvius

8. The biggest dome is the: (130)
K. Astrodome
D. Washington Capitol Building
N. St. Peter's (Vatican City)
S. Louisiana Superdome

If you have circled all the correct letters, you will spell out the name of an athlete. Who is this person and what is his record? (284)

(Answer on page 143)

# CRICKETERS

(Answers on page 143)

Each line in the problems below spelled out the name of a record-setting cricketer. Unfortunately, the apprentice upset the type, so that the letters in each vertical column became scrambled. But you can still find the correct names. For example, to spell TONY in the first problem, select the T in the first column, any of the O's in the second column, the N in the third column, and the Y in the fourth column. Complete this name, then find the other names as well.

1.
```
J O N L K E N K
J A H Y R U G D
T O U L L I I G
P O M N A O E O
J I H N H K C R
```

2.
```
W E H L I D R I E N
P R S L R H A O E G
J A T O L G L O U T
A E N N W E E D N E
L O L E Y I S M N S
```

3.
```
T E B E F Y T L M R N
P E D L R R O W B E D
R E C H Y T C E A E S
H O T C R H E R I S R
P I R E E H O A M A P
```

4.
```
H O W A R A P O V L E S
D D G H R D Y M O T N N
A N T I S C O F R O L N
E E N F T N Y B P E W D
G U D H O E Y E I A O Y
```

5.
```
E I L N N D B E U T M A S
W O L T E A L P A T L E N
W E W L L R F H U L O O N
D D O A I R M R L L S O N
L A N I A A D L E D T W N
```

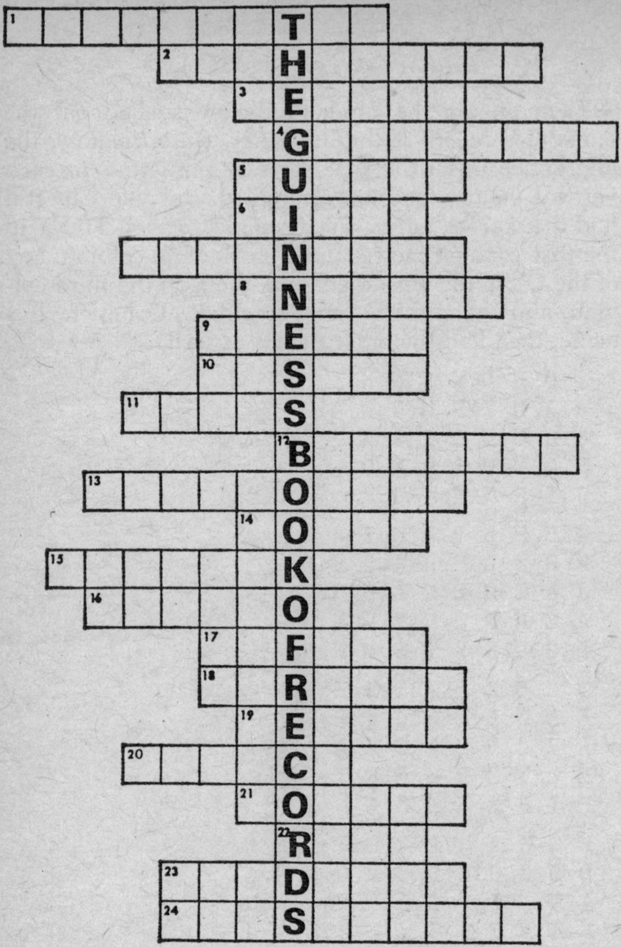
THE GUINNESS BOOK OF RECORDS

# A TOURIST'S ITINERARY

What city must a tourist visit to see each of the attractions mentioned below? Enter the name within the proper blocks on the opposite page. The names of well-known cities are used, even though the feature may be outside the city.

1. The largest wooden building. (117)
2. The largest library. (98)
3. A terminal of the Grand Canal. (125)
4. The largest painting in the United Kingdom. (87)
5. The largest roof. (120)
6. The spa accommodating the most visitors. (119)
7. The largest art gallery. (88)
8. The largest single canal lock. (126)
9. The largest operating Big Wheel. (121)
10. The largest dry dock. (131)
11. *La Gioconda.* (87)
12. The widest street. (206)
13. The largest mural. (89)
14. The worst traffic jams. (207)
15. The largest museum. (89)
16. The largest wine cellars. (122)
17. The oldest museum. (89)
18. The tallest self-supporting tower. (123)
19. The largest zoo collection. (54)
20. The largest Old Master. (87)
21. The hotel with the most rooms. (119)
22. The largest standing obelisk. (130)
23. The heaviest bell in use. (103)
24. The longest canal tunnel. (128)

(Answers on page 144)

# ANSWERS

## Guinness Party Quiz

1. 8 feet 11.1 inches
2. 1,069 lb.
3. 113 years 124 days
4. 26 feet
5. 8½ feet
6. 17½ feet
7. 18 feet 9¾ inches
8. 7¾ inches
9. 20 feet
10. 180 feet
11. 37½ feet (anaconda)
12. 366.2 feet
13. 112–113 feet (cypress)
14. 4.22 tons
15. 2 March
16. 1,250 feet 9 inches
17. 3,875
18. 3,212 feet
19. 21
20. 5
21. 48 hours 18 minutes
22. 83
23. 6,270 lb.
24. 21 feet
25. 6⅛ inches
26. 24 lb. 4 oz.
27. 1922
28. 25,000 miles
29. 136.4°F
30. —126.9°F

## Hyperbole

1. C ________ only 10.
2. B ________ only since 1901.
3. B ________ only £100.
4. A ________ only 25.78 m.p.h.
5. B ________ only 89.
6. C ________ only 1.
7. A ________ only 5 miles.
8. C ________ Lake Baykal.
9. A ________ only 1,800 miles.
10. C ________ only one.
11. C ________ only 7.
12. A ________ only about two-thirds of the way.
13. A ________ only 1,350 feet.
14. B ________ only one leg.
15. A ________ 42 days.
16. C ________ only 2,000.
17. B ________ only two.
18. C ________ only age 3.
19. B ________ only half that fast.
20. C ________ only 550 feet.

## Twenty-One

A. 12
B. 5
C. 19
D. 15
E. 1
F. 21
G. 10
H. 17
I. 8
J. 4
K. 7
L. 11
M. 20
N. 16
O. 2
P. 9
Q. 14
R. 6
S. 18

## A Birthday Treasure Hunt

1. Darts.
2. Gramophone.
3. In the Oxford English Dictionary.
4. Telephones.
5. In the bathroom.
6. Matches.
7. Draughts.
8. Car.
9. On a television program.
10. Globe.
11. Staircase.
12. Budgerigars.
13. Clock.
14. Piano.
15. Radio.
16. Calendar.

## Limericks

1. A professional living statue, he was wounded in the back by a man trying to prove to his wife that Fuqua wasn't real.

2. Schoolboy L. Vernon Vaughan sold the unique British Guiana one cent black on magenta stamp cheaply. It is now catalogued at £120,000.

3. Mills Darden was heavy, his wife slender. There was a difference of more than 65 stone in their weights.

## A Quickie Quiz

1. Angel.
2. Badminton Hall in Avon.
3. Armstrong and Aldrin *landed* simultaneously.
4. Their five children, including a set of twins, were all born on this date—which is also U.S. income tax deadline.
5. They may be able to hear higher tones.
6. Queensland life savers use them as protection against jellyfish.
7. The man after whom the Howard Libbey tree was named.
8. Built the Aswan Dam, which cut off some meanders.
9. This lake in Tibet has no name.
10. Federal employees may go home.
11. In China, particularly the *Cheng Ho*, around 1420.
12. She made a 360° roll.
13. It has a narrow gauge railway.
14. A chimpanzee.
15. The *Flyer I*.
16. Montreal will have a larger one.
17. It is in Paradise, Kentucky, U.S.A.
18. Parker Bros., chiefly for their game Monopoly.
19. A Ford Escort car.
20. 1974.
21. It is not on a river.
22. Born a king, he died at 4 days.
23. Peace.
24. United States.
25. He was only 31, so he would have been made a year older.
26. For sitting down—in traffic.
27. New York Police Department.
28. Many of them, when they were paroled or their terms expired.
29. Meal breaks.

30. Around the world, if legally obtained; if illegally, to prison.

31. It is only 26 inches wide.

32. Gravelly Hill.

33. Hyde Park Corner.

34. He would like to visit them, as these are the only countries and territories he has not seen.

35. Running.

36. They descended to the bottom of the ocean at its greatest depth.

37. He was attacked by owls.

38. Lees walked; Ball ran.

39. Lots of pain—and the bonds were never used.

40. She chose the money instead.

41. Circus Circus.

42. Hair straightener.

43. A super cluster of galaxies.

44. They might lose their clothes to a successful player.

45. On the moon.

46. It was struck by a boat.

47. She became too large for her tank, and was given her freedom. We refer to Gigi, the performing whale, not Gigi the world's fattest cat.

48. It would only last a split second.

49. The shortest alphabet.

50. He was legless.

51. He may have been an escaping prisoner.

## Painting Ladder

Mona, monk, mink, link, lint, list, Lisa.

## Speed Ladder

Swift, shift, shirt, short, shore (or snort), share (or snore), snare, snarl, snail.

## Mammal Ladder

Whale, shale, share, shore, short, shoot, scoot, scoop, stoop, strop, strap, straw, strew, shrew.

## Letter Cross Out

1. Gored
2. Tinned
3. Goes, bed, too
4. Hooked
5. Fred
6. Thinness
7. Hen
8. Gun
9. Ford
10. Thief
11. Hero
12. Inn
13. Hike
14. Bore
15. Ness

## Sets

1. These three points form the biggest landless triangle, in the South Pacific.
2. These racehorses ran the first quadruple dead heat.
3. And these four ran the only other quadruple dead heat.
4. These four Eskimos accompanied Peary on his Arctic polar exploration.
5. Only two heavyweight champions to retire, permanently, undefeated.
6. Three films for which Katherine Hepburn won starring Oscars.
7. The two most recorded songs.
8. Early forms of, respectively: football, polo, basketball, bridge, chess, golf, and lacrosse.
9. Names of the two primeval super-continents.
10. These are the most remote islands, the first inhabited, the second uninhabited.
11. Longest undebatable palindromes in English.
12. The longest words in the French, Croatian, Italian, Japanese, Russian, and Hungarian dictionaries.
13. Had the longest engagement.
14. Shared in the longest film kiss.
15. First films publicly shown.
16. Main performers in *The Golden Horseshoe Revue*, the record-holder for the most performances.
17. Siberian towns with the greatest temperature variations.
18. Asteroids that are in resonance with the earth.
19. The closest star to the sun, and the closest star visible to the unaided eye.
20. Spent the most time in space.
21. These are all United Kingdom surnames.
22. This was the total correspondence between Victor Hugo and his publisher concerning sales on his new book.
23. The largest battleships ever built—and sunk.

24. Their inventions made the computer possible.

25. Collectors of labels, bookmatch covers, and matchboxes.

26. Tied in an election.

27. Physicists whose work led to man-made fission.

28. The shortest murder trials, half a minute each.

29. These countries have no coinage.

30. All had to endure periods of prohibition of alcoholic beverages.

31. The gap in the world's longest highway.

32. Travelled the farthest from the earth.

33. The women who reached the highest altitude on a mountain.

34. Oldest bridegroom and bride.

35. United Kingdom beauty queens.

36. These are all one person, the 18th Duchess of Alba.

37. Each was awarded a bar to the Victoria Cross.

38. No bars have ever been issued.

39. These are the largest diamonds, cut and uncut respectively.

40. These horses ran at odds of 100 to 1 on.

41. These were the longest Roman roads in Britain.

## Brain Teaser

There are no seas on the moon, therefore, no sea level, so the answer to this portion is zero. When multiplying any sum by zero, the entire product is zero. So the answer is zero.

## Riddles

1. In Chinese the sound of thunder requires 52 strokes and is pronounced "ping."

2. The Cambodian alphabet has 74 letters.

3. Saturn's density is less than that of water.

4. Buddy Rich holds the record as the highest-paid drummer.

5. London and Paris are the largest settlements on Christmas Island in the Pacific.

6. The largest painting, *Panorama of the Mississippi*, was destroyed by fire.

7. Robert Liston amputated a limb in 33 seconds, but also cut off three of his assistant's fingers.

8. A hitch-hiker, he picked up more than six thousand rides, before catching a ride in a Rolls-Royce.

9. A Chinese typewriter, the Hoang, has nearly six thousand characters.

10. Al Capone, the gangster who called himself a second hand furniture dealer, grossed more than $100,000,000 in a year.

11. Emanuel Zacchini, a human cannonball, was replaced by his daughter Florinda, who was the same size.

12. Kathy Aylwin O'Driscoll's wedding cake had 27 tiers.

13. A professional blood donor, his rare type earned him a good income.

14. Vivian "Sailor Joe" Simmons was the most tattoed person.

15. She could see 20 times better than average.

## Strange Journeys

1. By earth orbit.
2. With the first true internal-combustion engined vehicle.
3. In an amphibious vehicle.
4. Unicycle.
5. Balloon.
6. Hot-air balloon.
7. By human-powered flight.
8. To the North Pole.
9. Walking backwards.
10. Swimming.
11. Continuous swimming.
12. Raft.
13. Hitch-hiking.
14. He was blown there by an explosion.
15. In free flight with a kite.
16. Stilts.
17. On a tightrope over Niagara Falls.
18. Walking on his hands.
19. Canoe.
20. On crutches.
21. To hit a golf ball.
22. He was blind.
23. Running backwards.
24. Underwater, with an air hose attached to his pilot boat.
25. Scuba.
26. Skis and parachute.
27. Skiing.
28. Roller skates.

## Scenic Acrostic

```
      R A F T
        N A M E
  E N G L I S H
      B E L L S
B O W L S
```

Angel Falls

## Sports Acrostic

```
        G R A I N
      L E O N I D
    S N O W F A L L
  P E A R L
        G E R M A N Y
    G R E Y H O U N D
```

George Rowley

## Giant Acrostic

```
R O W E D
O P A L
B A D M I N T O N
E E L
R O O S E V E L T
T O W E R
```

Robert Wadlow

## The Beginning and the End

1. The first heart transplant.
2. The first trans-Atlantic wireless signal.
3. The first aeroplane flight across the Channel.
4. The first trans-Atlantic flight.
5. The first non-stop trans-Atlantic flight.
6. The *Daily Mail* trans-Atlantic race.
7. The removal of London Bridge.
8. The largest sheep move.
9. The first crossing of the Arctic ice.
10. The first solo trans-Atlantic crossing by rowing.

## Yes or No Spelldown

1. Yes.
2. No, only two.
3. No, just under 12.
4. No, it is the run over which the Bayonne Bridge was built.
5. No, Mauna Kea.
6. Yes.
7. No, Mount Blanc.
8. Yes.
9. Yes.
10. Yes.
11. No, Methuselah.
12. Yes.
13. No, Vishnu.
14. No, a love song to a god.
15. No, Jupiter.
16. Yes.
17. Yes.
18. Yes.
19. No.
20. Yes.
21. Yes.
22. No, Canada.

23. No.
24. Yes.
25. Yes.
26. No, 5 feet 9 inches.
27. Yes.
28. No, larch.
29. No, about 37 times.
30. No, it is a starfish.
31. No, Chimborazo.
32. No, the Grand Banks.
33. Yes.
34. No.
35. No, Jupiter.
36. No, Andromeda.
37. Yes.
38. No, heroin.
39. Yes.
40. Yes.
41. No, *Ben Hur*.
42. Yes.
43. Yes.
44. No, shahtoosh.
45. No, Poland.
46. No, the Swiss Guard at the Vatican.
47. No.
48. Yes.
49. No, coloured glass.
50. Yes.
51. No, Queen Victoria.

**What's the Question?**

1. What were the first aeroplanes to fly around the world?

2. Why did Beverly Nina divorce some of her sixteen husbands?

3. What were Andrew Carnegie's favourite philanthropies?

4. Why was the Graf Zeppelin II more valuable to the Germans in peacetime than in wartime?

5. What series of obstacles was escape-artist Reynir Léossen able to overcome?

6. What, and for how long, slowed Big Ben in 1945?

7. What is reputedly the most haunted place?

8. What is the largest painting?

9. What work by a British artist brought the highest auction price? (By Thomas Gainsborough.)

10. What were the first words written in the sky?

11. What do the largest letters in the world spell?

12. What was the first recording to receive a real golden disc?

13. What is the longest running T.V. programme on B.B.C.?

14. What is the oldest wooden building in the world?

15. What was the earliest dam ever built?

16. In what field is the deepest penetration by man into the earth's crust?

17. Where is the largest artificial heap?

18. Why doesn't the *Aluminaut* descend as far as she is engineered to go?

19. What is accomplished by the oldest machinery (excluding clocks) in the United Kingdom?

20. For whose tomb was the largest slab of marble utilised?

21. What branch store has the largest merchandise turnover?

22. What catastrophe struck the British Museum in 1847?

23. What Italian political party had only one candidate?

24. Where was the last pitched land battle in Britain fought?

25. Where was the last invasion of Great Britain?

26. What was the shortest valid will? ("All to wife.")

27. Why did the people in Copenhagen visit the barber less often than normal?

28. What is the most severe unclassified road in Britain?

29. Where in Great Britain is it possible to drive on a surface road below sea level?

30. How was possible nuclear disaster averted?

31. How many steps are there in the Eiffel Tower?

32. What stream is arched by the oldest existing bridge?

33. What is the largest common in the United Kingdom?

34. How far can the beacons on the Empire State Building be seen?

35. What are the fastest rapids navigated?

36. What was the first all-talking film?

37. What is the largest book in the world?

38. Whose autograph is the most valuable?

39. How old is the Faversham Oyster Fishery Co.?

40. What is the highest motor road in Europe?

41. What is the name of the largest cable-laying ship?

42. What role earned Sean Connery a reported $13.5 million?

43. What island is the most northerly land?

44. What trophy is awarded for proficiency in tiddlywinks?

45. How do you qualify to swim in the largest landlocked swimming pool?

46. Why don't patriots in Bahrain and Qatar sing their national anthems?

## Match the Answers

| | | | |
|---|---|---|---|
| 1. K | 5. I | 9. D | 13. J |
| 2. C | 6. A | 10. H | 14. P |
| 3. F | 7. N | 11. L | 15. M |
| 4. G | 8. O | 12. E | 16. B |

## True/Plus/Minus

1. Plus (150)
2. True
3. Plus (2,119)
4. Minus (260)
5. Minus (51.5)
6. Minus (53.5)
7. True
8. Plus (66)
9. True
10. Plus (7½)
11. True
12. Minus (7,500)
13. Minus (93)
14. True
15. Plus (3.5)
16. True
17. Minus (161)
18. True
19. Plus (178)
20. Plus (123)
21. True
22. Minus (299)
23. Minus (4,400)
24. Minus (10)
25. Plus (4,920)
26. True
27. Minus (110)
28. Minus (6)
29. True
30. Plus (5,799)
31. True
32. Minus (126)
33. Minus (11 ft, 11 in)
34. True
35. Plus (27)
36. Minus (69)
37. Plus (34)
38. True
39. True
40. Plus (465)
41. Plus (192)
42. Minus (241)
43. Plus (over 25,000)
44. True
45. Plus (about 430,000)
46. True
47. Plus (223)
48. Plus (42,768)
49. Plus (35)
50. Minus (265)
51. True
52. Minus (200)
53. Minus (231)
54. True
55. Plus (325)
56. Minus (310)
57. True
58. Minus (27)

59. Plus (over 4)
60. Plus (33)
61. Minus (47)
62. Plus (1,306)
63. Minus (15)
64. Minus (11)
65. True
66. True
67. Minus (11)
68. True
69. Minus (6)
70. True

## Square of Fame

1. Winston Churchill
2. Babe Ruth
3. Isaac Newton
4. Pablo Picasso
5. Harry Houdini
6. Primo Carnera
7. Gertrude Ederle
8. Charles Lindbergh
9. Valentina Tereshkova
10. Jacqueline Cochran
11. Tenzing Norkhay
12. Ivan Turgenev
13. James Ross
14. Edmund Halley
15. Joseph Niépce
16. John Masefield
17. Ramu
18. Richard Nixon

| | | | | | | | | | | | | | | |
|---|---|---|---|---|---|---|---|---|---|---|---|---|---|---|
| E | N | Y | A | H | K | Z | N | L | L | S | [3] I | [9] V | A | L |
| V | E | G | R | O | R | I | E | [11] T | I | A | N | E | N | E |
| S | E | L | U | N | G | N | R | C | H | A | C | W | T | I |
| L | I | R | T | N | A | [1] W | U | H | C | V | A | T | A | N |
| [14] E | N | A | H | [8] C | V | I | T | O | N | O | N | O | T | E |
| D | D | B | E | [10] J | [12] I | N | S | E | C | K | H | S | E | R |
| M | U | N | R | A | C | Q | O | S | P | E | I | N | D | R |
| R | A | D | G | L | E | U | [15] J | E | P | H | N | I | H | A |
| R | [5] H | H | H | I | N | E | N | M | E | S | O | X | C | I |
| Y | H | A | L | L | O | C | A | A | O | R | N | E | [7] G | [18] R |
| D | O | U | D | E | C | H | R | [13] J | S | R | T | R | R | L |
| L | I | N | I | Y | A | B | R | I | S | U | E | D | E | E |
| E | A | M | O | H | [4] P | L | [6] P | M | O | D | E | R | E | B |
| I | [17] R | U | [16] J | N | O | O | P | I | C | N | E | U | T | A |
| F | E | S | A | M | S | S | A | C | A | R | R | A | H | [2] B |

## A High I.Q. Test

1. Greenland may be several islands covered with an ice-cap.

2. It is claimed that the harnessing of the tides serves to slow the rotation of the earth.

3. They were forced to re-evaluate the length of their time unit, the second.

4. Yes. The towers were built with their tops 1⅝ inches out of parallel to allow for the curvature of the earth.

5. Every day it sweeps up cosmic dust and meteoric debris, possibly as much as 40,000 tons.

6. There was no subsequent North Pole expedition for many years. Further, the South Pole is on land while the North Pole is on drifting sea ice.

7. Among the larger, familiar things it is. But seeds of the lupin plant have germinated after 10,000 years or more.

8. A meteorite in Mexico from the Allende fall. It is possible for a meteorite to be older than the earth itself.

9. Although Pluto is usually farther away, at certain times its more elliptical orbit creeps inside Neptune's more circular orbit.

10. It can be used to bore holes.

11. Theoretically they would disappear before they exist.

12. Very easily. Remember these recurring figures, 142857. The correct answer is 3.142857142857142-857 . . .

## Complete the Set

1. Sulphur . . . the ingredients for gunpowder.
2. Electricity Council . . . the western enterprises employing the most capital.
3. Horse . . . the probable order of their domestication.
4. China . . . the countries having land boundaries with the U.S.S.R.
5. Rwanda . . . the poorest countries.
6. Camel . . . a Bedouin wedding feast.
7. Sabre . . . fencing weapons.
8. Amazon . . . possibly the longest watercourse.
9. The length of the Panama Canal . . . the unique swimming achievement of Mihir Sen.

## Zero Quiz Game

1. 2
2. 6
3. 7
4. 5
5. 4
6. 8
7. 6
8. 10
9. 5
10. 5
11. 2
12. 6
13. 9
14. 8
15. 6
16. 3
17. 5
18. 3
19. 9
20. 100
21. 6
22. 5
23. 6
24. 3
25. 4
26. 8
27. 6
28. 8
29. 3
30. 6
31. 9
32. 3
33. 3
34. 5
35. 3
36. 8
37. 6
38. 8
39. 7
40. 8
41. 3
42. 5
43. 3
44. None
45. 4
46. 6
47. 12
48. 6
49. 5
50. 4
51. 6
52. 3

# Crossword of the Greatest

## Easy-to-Hard Cryptograms

1. Reverse the order of the words:
THE QUEEN ELIZABETH WAS THE LARGEST PASSENGER LINER. (137)

2. Space letters correctly:
THE TALLEST INHABITED BUILDING IS SEARS TOWER. (116)

3. Reverse the order of the word groups, then space correctly:
AUGSB URGCA THEDR ALHAS THEOL DESTS TAINE DGLAS S.
AUGSBURG CATHEDRAL HAS THE OLDEST STAINED GLASS. (212)

4. Reverse the sentence:
RON YAM LGL ORK GEJ ISI THH EHG IGF HEE STD BRC IDB GEA.
Cross out every third letter and space correctly:
RO YA LG OR GE IS TH EH IG HE ST BR ID GE.
ROYAL GORGE IS THE HIGHEST BRIDGE. (124)

5. Drop each first letter, then space correctly:
LUCI AZAR ATEW ASTH ELIG HTES TADU LTHU MAN.
LUCIA ZARATE WAS THE LIGHTEST ADULT HUMAN. (11)

6. Reverse the letters in every other group, then space correctly:
SWEDE NHAST HELAR GESTO RECAR RIER.
SWEDEN HAS THE LARGEST ORE CARRIER. (139)

7. Stagger the letters as shown below, then read across the lines:

```
T     H     E     E     I    F
 F     E     L     T     O     W
  E     R     H     A     S     A
   F     I     V     E     I     N
    C     H     S     W     A     Y
```

THEEIF FELTOW ERHASA FIVEIN CHSWAY.

THE EIFFEL TOWER HAS A FIVE-INCH SWAY. (123)

8. Reverse the letters in the second half of the message:

LGTIGOTSHLICTIK.

Stagger these letters with the letters of the first half of the message:

A I H N N B L I<br>
L G T I G O T S

A A F N H H C<br>
H L I C T I K

A LIGHTNING BOLT IS A HALF INCH THICK. (67)

9. Arrange in two-letter groups, then reverse the letters in each group and space correctly:

HT RE DE OR KC AM ED HT SE OL EW TS AP SS GA E.

TH ER ED RO CK MA DE TH ES LO WE ST PA SS AG E.

THE *RED ROCK* MADE THE SLOWEST PASSAGE. (140)

10. Reverse the letters in every second group:

SAYNR AIIAR HLAIS NTEHH EALSA ARTGW EOSMT IWNAU TTEER FWLHI EGEHL T.

Divide into groups of two letters:

SA YN RA II AR HL AI SN TE HH EA LS AA RT GW EO SM TI WN AU TT EE RF WL HI EG EH LT.

The first message is found by reading the first letters in each set:

SYRIAHASTHELARGESTWATER WHEEL.

SYRIA HAS THE LARGEST WATER WHEEL. (131)

The second message is found by reading the second letters in each set:

ANAIRLINEHASATWOMINUTE FLIGHT.

AN AIRLINE HAS A TWO-MINUTE FLIGHT. (151)

## Around the World

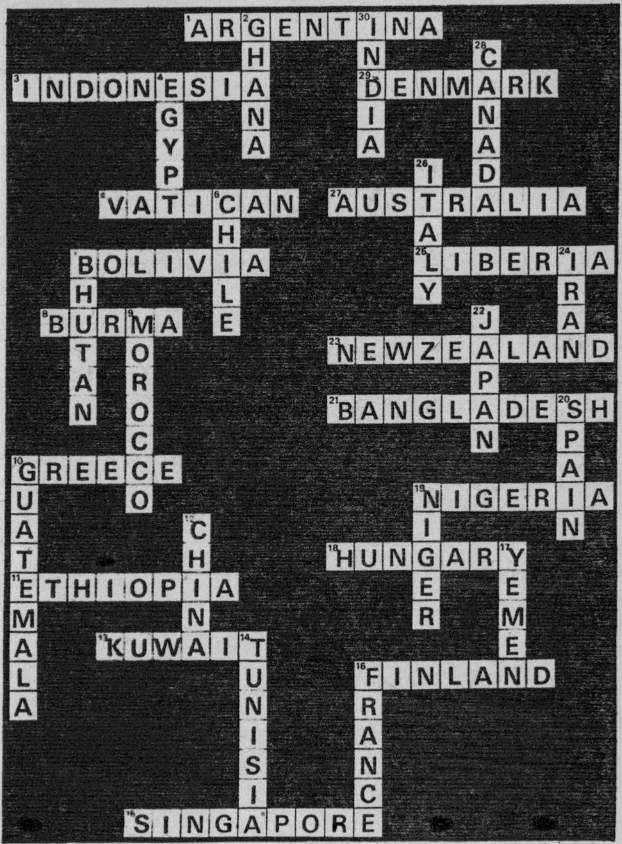


## Find the Bracket

| | | | | | | |
|---|---|---|---|---|---|---|
| 1. C | 8. B | 15. E | 22. E | 29. C | 36. A | 43. B |
| 2. B | 9. A | 16. E | 23. E | 30. C | 37. A | 44. B |
| 3. E | 10. C | 17. D | 24. D | 31. D | 38. E | 45. A |
| 4. B | 11. D | 18. A | 25. C | 32. A | 39. D | 46. B |
| 5. A | 12. B | 19. B | 26. A | 33. B | 40. B | 47. B |
| 6. C | 13. C | 20. E | 27. B | 34. E | 41. E | 48. D |
| 7. D | 14. A | 21. C | 28. C | 35. A | 42. D | 49. B |
| | | | | | | 50. D |

## Short Rebuses

1. KEY + TOE + HOLE − EYE + WEB − TWO + RUG − BUG = KOEHLER
2. BUN + FORD = BUNFORD
3. HOP + KNIFE + CRANES − FERN − ACE = HOPKINS
4. CAMP + BELL = CAMPBELL
5. LAMB + HEART + MICE − HAM − ICE = LAMBERT
6. BEAR − EAR + HAIR + DOG − HOG = BAIRD
7. TREE + VINE + THICK − KNEE + KITE − TIE = TREVITHICK
8. PALM + MOTHER − MOTH = PALMER
9. BEE + HAND − AND + BAND − BED = BEHAN
10. GO + ART + STONE − SEAT = GORTON

## Sports and Games Personalities

1. Alice Legh, archery
2. Dawn Fraser, swimming
3. Jim Pike, darts
4. Arthur Whitford, gymnastics
5. Edmund Hillary, mountaineering
6. Peter Sprogis, basketball
7. Garfield Sobers, cricket
8. Ted Drake, football (Association)
9. Charlotte Dod, lawn tennis
10. Michael Bull, pole vault
11. Ross Cleverly, boxing
12. Jonathan Penrose, chess
13. Patrick Sercu, cycling
14. Gillian Sheen, fencing
15. Bobby Hull, ice hockey
16. Tom Haliburton, golf

17. John Cobb, motor racing
18. Stuart Mackenzie, sculling
19. Geoffrey Liddiard, bowling (tenpin)
20. Jack Holden, cross-country running
21. Mick the Miller, greyhound racing
22. Jim Redman, motorcycling
23. Tulyar, horse racing
24. Paavo Nurmi, track
25. Rixi Markus, contract bridge
26. David Watkins, football (Rugby League)
27. Walter Lindrum, billiards
28. Heatherbloom, equestrian jumping
29. Patricia Tipper, ice skating
30. Paul Withers, polo

## Incongruous Members

1. One person speaks Manx; the answer to the others is zero. Nobel was a bachelor. The curtain collapsed before the first performance of *As You Like It.* The earth is believed to have passed through the tail of Haley's Comet; and some supposed meteorites may have been comets.

2. E is incongruous. The others made the longest self-supported sled journey, across Greenland.

3. D is not an event of the Modern Pentathlon.

4. D is non-poisonous.

5. B is an earthen dam, the others concrete.

6. D is a cantilever bridge, the others suspension.

7. D is not one of the Seven Wonders of the Ancient World.

8. C is a submarine, the others famous liners.

9. A and B were carved out of sapphire. Ford will have to wait.

10. The largest sculpture is of Confederate leaders, so A does not belong.

11. A and B made the first mechanical clock.

12. D uses standard gauge.

13. A is not one of the islands of the notorious French penal colony.

14. There is no Nobel prize for C.

15. I is the only item that was *not* found in the stomach of a particular patient.

16. A did not achieve the highest speed reached by man.

17. A and B are tribes that can count to 3. C cannot.

## Three-to-Three Maze

The number is 3.141592653589793, which is the value of pi ($\pi$) carried to 15 decimals, or 999,985 fewer than the 1,000,000 places of pi which have been calculated by computer.

## Ten Digits

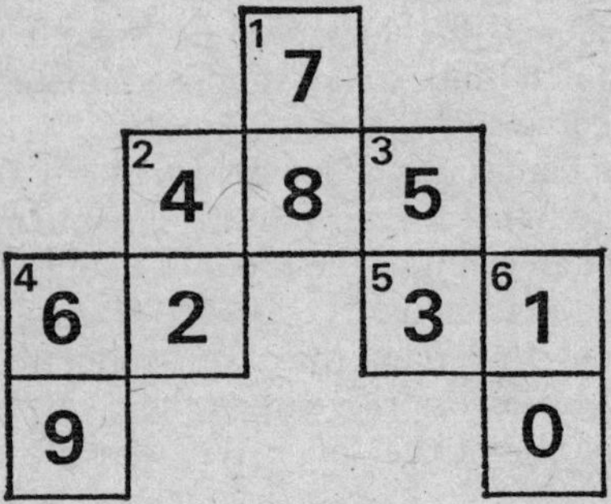

| | | | | |
|---|---|---|---|---|
| | | [1]5 | | |
| | [2]1 | 8 | [3]4 | |
| | 9 | | 7 | |
| [4]3 | 6 | | [5]2 | 0 |

| | | | | |
|---|---|---|---|---|
| | [1]1 | 0 | [2]2 | |
| [3]8 | 6 | ■ | [4]4 | 9 |
| | [5]3 | 7 | 5 | |

| | | | | | |
|---|---|---|---|---|---|
| [1]9 | | | | | [2]2 |
| [3]6 | [4]8 | | | [5]7 | 4 |
| | [6]1 | 0 | 3 | 5 | |

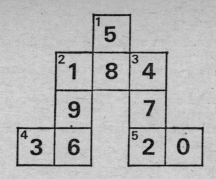

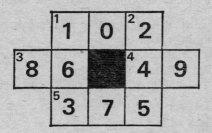

## Anagrams

I. Each man went around the world in the manner described:

1. Wiley Post was the first to fly alone around the world.
2. Elgen Long was the first to fly alone around the world across the poles.
3. Juan Sebastion led Magellan's men home from the first circumnavigation of the world.
4. Joshua Slocum was the first to sail alone around the world.
5. John Guzzwell circumnavigated the globe in the smallest boat.
6. Edward Beach led the first submarine crew around the world.
7. Robin Knox-Johnston was the first to sail alone around the world non-stop.
8. Yuriy Gagarin was the first to orbit the earth in a satellite.

II. 1. Black widow.
2. Funnel web.
3. Jockey.
4. Button.
5. Podadora.
6. Brown recluse.

These are all spiders that have been charged with fatalities.

III. 1. Quail eggs.
2. Iranian caviar.
3. Crayfish tails.
4. Roast lamb.
5. Roast peacock.
6. Foie gras.
7. Fig rings.
8. Raspberry sweet champagne sherbet.
9. Wines.

This was the menu at the most expensive banquet, in Iran. Wish you were there?

IV. 1. Jean Paul Getty.
2. John MacArthur.
3. Haroldson L. Hunt.
4. Daniel Ludwig.
5. John D. Rockefeller.
6. Howard Hughes.
7. Henry Ford.
8. Andrew Mellon.
9. H. Ross Perot.
All are or were American billionaires.

## Places to Hide

1. Lundy Island, off the Devon coast.
2. Dead Room, Murray Hill, New Jersey.
3. There have been no cases in England or Wales in four decades.
4. Anywhere except New Guinea.
5. Mt. Wai-'ale'ale, Hawaii.
6. Baruduksum, Tibet.
7. Wulumuch'i, China, the large town most remote from the sea.
8. Gibraltar.
9. Sweden.
10. Netherlands.
11. Israel.
12. United States.
13. Deep underground for five years.
14. Spain.
15. Jordan.
16. Liechtenstein was the first to abolish it.
17. Ireland has the greatest calorific consumption (but will there be any left?).
18. Cape Wrath, Sutherland.
19. Shore of the Dead Sea.
20. Niger Republic.

21. Tasaday tribe, Philippines.
22. Ireland.
23. Switzerland.
24. West Germany.
25. Bishop Rock, Isle of Scilly.

## Opposites

1. The most common and the rarest blood types.
2. Possibly the shortest and the longest rivers.
3. The longest liner, and the biggest sailing vessel.
4. The highest place a fixed-wing aeroplane has landed, and the lowest.
5. These were the most and the least profitable British firms.
6. The most crossed international border, and the least.
7. The northernmost town, and the southernmost.
8. The northernmost capital, and the southernmost.
9. Have the highest bank rate, and the lowest.
10. The first is natural, the second artificial.
11. The bomb was known as "Little Boy"; eight-year-old Joy Foster was a little girl.
12. The most disciplined football club, and the least.
13. These were opponents in the Battle of Lepanto, the greatest ancient naval action.
14. The first holds a torch; the second a sword.
15. Though considered the world's most valuable painting, Lisa's husband considered it worthless.
16. Xenon is the element with the most isotopes; hydrogen the fewest.
17. Ubyx is the language with the most consonants; Rotokas the fewest.
18. The first swam from France to England; the second from England to France.
19. Monaco has the highest per capita number of telephones; Upper Volta the fewest.
20. The first eat the most meat; the second the least.

## Double Answers

1. Daisy and Violet Hilton and the London Hilton.
2. John Stuart Mill and a (wind) mill.
3. *The Adventure of the Lion's Mane.*
4. Mount Washington and the Washington Monument.
5. Newton.
6. Venus.
7. Autolite-Ford Parts Redistribution Center and Ford Parts Centre.
8. Desmond Guinness and Guinness Brewery.
9. Orchid Ballroom and orchid.
10. Disney World and Walt Disney.
11. Moat.
12. Crystal Palace and crystal.
13. The Swan, and swan.
14. Queen Mary.
15. Steamboat.
16. Apollo XI.
17. Church Hill and Winston Churchill.
18. Sirius.
19. Squash rackets and squash court.
20. *The £1,000,000 Bank-Note.*
21. *Normandie* and Normandy.
22. Jules Léotard and leotard.
23. Ignace Jan Paderewski.
24. Rockets, Rockettes.
25. Alice Stevenson and Robert Louis Stevenson.
26. *White Christmas.*

## A Secret Message

1. J
2. H
3. B
4. G
5. I
6. O
7. M
8. F
9. P
10. D
11. E
12. L
13. A
14. N
15. C
16. K

The secret message: Police handy, chums.

## Mark's Maze

The letters to be checked are B, C, E, F, I, and K.

## Truth or Consequences

1. Yes.
2. Bottle.
3. Tapestry.
4. Flag.
5. South.
6. Telephones.
7. Asquith.
8. Louis XIV.
9. Emigrate.
10. Horse.
11. Antarctic.
12. Lightning.
13. The same.
14. Indoor.
15. Typist.
16. Shareholders.
17. Assets.
18. White.
19. France.
20. Parliament.
21. Mount Everest.
22. Mercury.

## Mathematical True or False

1.

| | | |
|---|---|---|
| 278 | 157 | The correct answers to the false statements are 195 and 756. |
| 117 | 109 | |
| 14 | | |
| —143 | | |
| 266 | 266 | |

2.

| | | |
|---|---|---|
| 1300 | 315 | The correct answers to the false statements are 191, 444, 136 and 152. |
| 420 | 689 | |
| | 611 | |
| | 105 | |
| 1720 | 1720 | |

3.

| | | |
|---|---|---|
| 408 | 265 | The correct answers to the false statements are 185, 100, 328 and 145. |
| 365 | 65 | |
| | 143 | |
| | 300 | |
| 773 | 773 | |

## Seesaw

1. Quetzalcóatl is bigger than the Great Pyramid.
2. A pig is heavier than the heaviest man.
3. A cake is heavier than an elephant.
4. A polar bear is heavier than a tiger.
5. An ostrich is heavier than a St. Bernard.
6. A gorilla is heavier than a giant clam.
7. A rabbit is heavier than a chicken.
8. A sphinx moth is heavier than a bee hummingbird.
9. Three blue whales are heavier than an aeroplane (note that the fulcrum is off centre).
10. A cut diamond is heavier than a spider.
11. A kite is heavier than a car.
12. Brachiosaurus is heavier than a bulldozer.
13. A cabbage is heavier than a cauliflower.
14. A pearl is heavier than a potato.
15. A shark is heavier than a string ball.

## Crossword of the Smallest

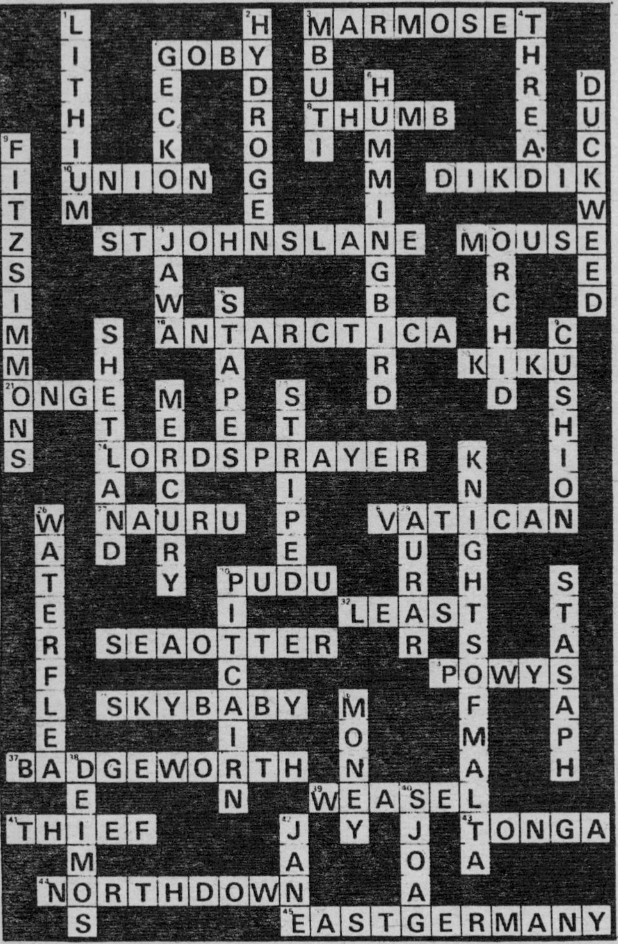

**Multiple Choice Ship**

NIMITZ

The *Nimitz*, an aircraft carrier, is the largest naval vessel.

## Multiple Choice Insect

CICADA

Although known for its many years below ground in the larva stage, the cicada holds the world's record as the noisiest insect.

## Multiple Choice Athlete

NICKLAUS

Jack Nicklaus is the golfer who has won the most major titles.

## Cricketers

1. Jim Laker (259), John Reid (258), Tony Lock (259), John King (261), Paul Hugo (261)
2. Wally Grout (260), Peter Heine (258), John Wisden (259), Arnold Long (260), Leslie Ames (260)
3. Tich Freeman (258), Percy Holmes (258), Robert Crisp (259), Hedley Taber (260), Peter Howard (260)
4. Hugh Tayfield (258), Denis Compton (257), Anthony Brown (260), Edward Pooley (260), Godfrey Evans (260)
5. Edwin Alletson (257), Walter Fellows (258), William Pullen (261), Donald Bradman (258), Leonard Hutton (257)

## A Tourist's Itinerary

1. Wellington
2. Washington
3. Peking
4. Greenwich
5. Munich
6. Vichy
7. Leningrad
8. Antwerp
9. Vienna
10. Lisbon
11. Paris
12. Brasilia
13. Mexico City
14. Tokyo
15. New York
16. Cape Town
17. Oxford
18. Toronto
19. Berlin
20. Venice
21. Moscow
22. Rome
23. Mandalay
24. Marseilles